lonely 🌐 planet

POCKET

MUNICH

TOP EXPERIENCES • LOCAL LIFE

T0021283

MARC DI DUCA

Contents

Plan Your Trip

Dianatempel, Hofgarten (p53)
WESTEND61/GETTY IMAGES ©

Explore Munich 37

Worth a Trip

Survival Guide 143

COVID-19

We have re-checked every business in this book before publication to ensure that it is still open after the COVID-19 outbreak. However, the economic and social impacts of COVID-19 will continue to be felt long after the outbreak has been contained, and many businesses, services and events referenced in this guide may experience ongoing restrictions. Some businesses may be temporarily closed, have changed their opening hours and services, or require bookings; some unfortunately could have closed permanently. We suggest you check with venues before visiting for the latest information. Check https://reopen.europa.eu for current restrictions in EU member countries.

Munich's Top Experiences

Tour the Wittelsbach rulers' spectacular Residenz (p40)

CRISTI POPESCU/SHUTTERSTOCK © BAYERISCHE SCHLÖSSERVERWALTUNG WWW.SCHLOESSER.BAYERN.DE

Raise a *Mass* (or two) at Oktoberfest (p138)

Watch the Glockenspiel on Marienplatz (p42)

Allow plenty of time for the Kunstareal's art museums (p64)

Picnic in the Englischer Garten (p84)

MATEJ KASTELIC/SHUTTERSTOCK ©

ANNE CZICHOS/SHUTTERSTOCK ©

Learn all about the city at Münchner Stadtmuseum (p44)

Pay your respects at KZ-Gedenkstätte Dachau (p80)

BERNARD BARROSO/SHUTTERSTOCK ©

TRABANTOS/SHUTTERSTOCK ©

Admire Schloss Nymphenburg's collection of women's portraits (p120)

See how BMWs are made (p124)

ANTON_IVANOV/SHUTTERSTOCK ©

YURII ANDREICHYN/SHUTTERSTOCK ©

Relive Germany's FIFA World Cup victory at Olympiapark (p122)

Spend a day at the palaces of Schleissheim (p100)

Put the kids in a mouse wheel at Deutsches Museum (p104)

Dining Out

RALF MENACHE/GETTY IMAGES ©

Munich has southern Germany's most exciting restaurant scene. In Munich's kitchens the best dishes make use of fresh regional, seasonal and organic ingredients. The Bavarian capital is also the best place between Vienna and Paris for internationally flavoured dining, especially for Italian, Afghan, Vietnamese and Turkish food, and even vegetarians can look forward to something other than noodles and salads.

Traditional Bavarian

Bavarian cuisine is hearty and filling. Menus are packed with pork, sausages, veal and river fish, and many dishes are accompanied by dumplings, thick sauces and sauerkraut. One dish you won't find anywhere else is *Weisswurst,* white veal sausages eaten for breakfast with a pretzel and a jug of wheat beer.

International Cuisine & Vegetarian Options

You don't have to be in the Bavaria metropolis for long to realise that the Bavarians are bonkers about Italian food, while Thai, Vietnamese, Korean and Indian food is becoming increasingly popular. Several Afghan restaurants serve the local Afghani population. Vegetarians are well catered for in a few specialist restaurants.

Fine Dining

Munich is an affluent city that can easily support tens of fine dining establishments, gourmet bistros and Michelin-starred eateries. It goes perhaps without saying that prices are astronomical, standards high and portions minuscule. There's also no chance of getting a seat in any of Munich's top-notch nosheries without booking months ahead.

LUISA FUMI/SHUTTERSTOCK ©

Best Bavarian

Fraunhofer Character-packed, olde-worlde dining room and filling fare. (p54)

Wirtshaus in der Au The speciality here is the dumpling – they'll even to teach you how to make them. (p113)

Weinhaus Neuner Pair your Alpine food with great wines. (p57)

Bratwurstherzl Franconian sausages in the heart of the Bavarian capital. (p53)

Best International

Chopan Arguably Munich's best Afghan restaurant. (p134)

Cochinchina Asian-fusion cuisine set in deepest Schwabing. (p92)

Il Mulino One of Munich's first Italian restaurants and still one of the best. (p77)

Best Fine Dining

Esszimmer The city's best restaurant with two Michelin twinklers. (p135)

Galleria Top-notch Italian job in the city centre. (p57)

Tantris Groovy gourmet eating in northern Schwabing. (p94)

Showroom Gourmet neighbourhood eatery near the Deutsches Museum. (p113)

Best Vegetarian

Prinz Myshkin Widely regarded as Bavaria's best veggie restaurant. (p54)

Vegelangelo Small, intimate vegetarian restaurant with set weekend menus. (p55)

Bar Open

Munich is a great place for boozers. Raucous beer halls, snazzy hotel lounges, chestnut-canopied beer gardens, DJ bars, designer cocktail temples – the variety is huge. And no matter where you are, you won't be far from an enticing cafe to get a caffeine-infused pick-me-up. Munich has some of Europe's best nightclubs with exciting venues for almost every musical taste.

HENGLEIN AND STEETS/GETTY IMAGES ©

Beer Halls & Gardens

No visit to Munich would be complete without an evening in a traditional beer hall or, in summer, a beer garden. The Bavarian capital has some of the best beer in the world and some of the best pubs in which to enjoy it. The Hofbräuhaus is the mothership of all beer halls, but there are plenty of other less touristy spots across the city.

Clubbing

Munich boasts the best clubbing in southern Germany with cutting-edge nightspots attracting internationally renown DJs. There's something for absolutely every taste and hairstyle in this town but things don't usually get going until midnight and finish at breakfast time.

Bars & Cafes

The city centre teems with characterful bars and cafes, especially in Schwabing and south of the Altstadt. You'll find everything from grungy student dives with second-hand furniture to twee coffee-and-cake spots for well-healed grandmas and everything in between.

MARIIA GOLOVIANKO/SHUTTERSTOCK ©

Best Beer Halls

Hofbräuhaus Not a beer hall, *the* beer hall, though too touristy for some. (p59)

Augustiner-Grossgaststätte Large historical tavern on the main shopping street. (p58)

Alter Simpl Once the local of Thomas Mann and Herman Hesse (p77)

Hofbräukeller Wood-panelled beer hall serving Hofbräu beers. (p115)

Best Beer Gardens

Hirschgarten With 8000 seats, there's no risk of queueing for a pew. (p136)

Chinesischer Turm Pea-green benches and tables swirl around a faux Chinese pagoda. (p95; pictured above right)

Hirschau Superb outdoor quaffing spot in the north of the English Garden. (p97)

Biergarten Muffatwerk Alternative beer garden with cool music and vegetarian food. (p115)

Park-Cafe Small, almost-tourist-free spot in the old Botanical Gardens. (p77)

Best Clubbing

Pacha Dance till sunrise at one of Munich's hottest clubs. (p57)

milchundbar Long-standing favourite among Munich's serious clubbers. (p57)

Rote Sonne Weekend dance spot for fans of electric sounds. (p59)

Harry Klein Possibly the best Elektro-club in Europe. (p78)

Best Bars & Cafes

Schumann's Bar Long-established and busy meeting point day and night. (p57)

Trachtenvogl Eclectic cafe attracting a mixed crowd. (p58)

Baader Café Hip drinking spot south of the Altstadt. (p59)

Schlosscafé im Palmenhaus Light refreshments in the old glasshouse at Schloss Nymphenburg. (p135)

Treasure Hunt

Munich is a fun and sophisticated place to shop that goes far beyond chains and department stores. If you want those, head to Neuhauser Strasse and Kaufingerstrasse. Southeast of there, Sendlinger Strasse has smaller and somewhat more individual stores. The Glockenbachviertel and Schwabing have many intriguing stores specialising in vintage clothing, books and antiques.

Souvenirs

From fridge magnets to felt hats, and Bayern Munich memorabilia to sturdy German design items, mementos from your trip to the Bavarian capital will be easy to find, especially in the city centre. The most common souvenirs are beer mugs and other beer paraphernalia – more refined items include Nymphenburg porcelain and German glassware.

Clothing

As across Europe, vintage clothing is all the rage and Munich has several upcycling stores selling used attire. Prices may be slightly steeper than you are used to back home but the quality is very high. A common souvenir from Munich is a folk costume either of the cheap variety for beer-hall frolics or the expensive real deal.

Flea Markets & Second-Hand

Germany has no charity shops so people get rid of their junk at huge flea markets that normally take place on weekends at large open venues. There's something particularly exciting about rummaging through pre-loved items in a foreign country and Munich offers plenty of opportunities to do so. Munich also has one of the best second-hand English bookshops in central Europe.

LUISA FUMI/SHUTTERSTOCK ®

Souvenirs

Manufactum Solid, last-forever German design for house and garden. (p60)

Porzellan Manufaktur Nymphenburg Factory shop of Munich's well-known porcelain factory. (p137)

Clothing

Loden-Frey Traditional clothing at high prices. (p61)

Holareidulijö Used Lederhosen and Dirndl. (p79)

Pick & Weight High-quality vintage clothing sold by the kilo. (p97)

Flea Markets & Second-Hand

Flohmarkt im Olympiapark Second-hand frenzy at the Olypmpic Park. (p136)

Munich Readery Germany's largest range of second-hand books in English. (p78)

Words' Worth Books Stock up on English reading material. (p97)

Outdoor Equipment

If you are visiting Munich en route to adventure in the Alps or have just forgotten your mac, Munich has two excellent outdoor stockists selling absolutely anything you might need in the wild or on an urban sightseeing trek. The unsurpassed Globe-trotter (p60) and the more sports-oriented Schuster (p61) are both in the city centre.

Show Time

ETIENJONES/SHUTTERSTOCK ©

As you might expect from a major metropolis, Munich's entertainment scene is lively and multifaceted, though not particularly edgy. You can hobnob with high society at the opera or a classical music concert, catch a flick alfresco, foot tap to the rhythm in a jazz club or watch one of Germany's best football (soccer) teams triumph in a futuristic stadium.

Opera & Classical Music

There's plenty of high-brow action in the Bavarian capital, especially for fans of opera and classical music. Check out the listings at the Gasteig, Nationaltheater (pictured above left), the Staatstheater am Gärtnerplatz and the Prinzregententheater to find out what's on. Booking well ahead is advised.

Live Music

Munich has its fair share of jazz clubs, live-music venues and concert halls. Big acts have up until now performed at the Gasteig, but the ageing building is undergoing a complete renovation. Until then, performances will be at **Gasteig HP8** (Hans-Pressinger-Strasse 4–8, Sendling), 4km southwest, across the Isar.

Cinema & Theatre

Central Munich has everything from modern multiplexes to golden-age cinema theatres showing obscure local movies. For show information check any of the listings publications. Theatre is an impenetrable world for the non-German speaker and there are few performances in English.

Football

As well as being Germany's top football (soccer) team, FC Bayern München can usually be found come spring playing in the latter stages of the UEFA Champions League. They play at the Allianz Arena but you generally have to book tickets well in advance to see these sports stars in action.

ANAHTIRIS/SHUTTERSTOCK ©

Best Opera & Classical Music

Bayerische Staatsoper Arguably Germany's top opera company. (p60)

BR Symphonieorchester One of Bavaria's best orchestras. (p109)

Münchner Philharmoniker Munich's top orchestra performs at the Isarphilharmonie at Gasteig HP8. (p116)

Best Live Music

Jazzbar Vogler Top Altstadt night out. (p60)

Jazzclub Unterfahrt im Einstein The city's best place to listen to jazz. (p116)

Best Cinema & Theatre

Museum-Lichtspiele Oddball independent cinema showing films in English. (p116)

Bayerisches Staatsschauspiel Performing theatre classics at a number of Munich venues. (p52)

Münchner Kammerspiele Provocative interpretations of the classics plus works by contemporary playwrights. (p59)

Staatstheater am Gärtnerplatz Revamped in 2015 and once again putting on light opera, musicals and dance. (p60)

Cinema One of the few picture houses in Bavaria showing films in English. (p78)

Best Sport

FC Bayern München Germany's top football club. (p73)

Art

Munich is a world-class powerhouse when it comes to art. The city offers everything from gilt-edge contemporary to old masters. The Kunstareal is southern Germany's top arts hotspot with four internationally renowned art museums vying for visitors' attention. Other smaller galleries examine local art movements and styles.

Pre-19th-Century Art

Munich has some suberb collections of ancient, medieval, and Renaissance art, spread across several institutions. Everything from Greek statuary and Gothic church sculpture, to old Dutch masters and baroque frescoes can be found in the City of Art and Beer.

19th- & 20th-Century Art

As an arts destination, the Bavarian capital really excels when it comes to the art of the last two centuries. Not only do Munich's art museums display internationally famous works, the city also produced its own art movements and styles, most notably a local version of art nouveau. Some of the most respected artists of the early 20th century resided in Munich.

Contemporary Art

The contemporary scene is well represented in Munich with a couple of galleries dedicated just to today's art and installations.

LESTERTAIR/SHUTTERSTOCK ©

Best Pre-19th-Century Art

Alte Pinakothek Old European Masters in the Kunstareal. (p65)

Antikensammlungen Greek and Roman art on the Königsplatz. (p73)

Glyptothek Ludwig I's collection of Greek and Roman art. (p75)

Bayerisches National-museum Art galore from many different ages. (p89; pictured)

Best 19th- & 20th-Century Art

Sammlung Schack 19th-century Romantic art in a former embassy building. (p109)

Lenbachhaus Gallery devoted to the Blue Rider movement of the early 20th century. (p73)

Neue Pinakothek Van Gogh et al at Munich's best art museum. (p66)

Pinakothek der Moderne Picasso and other modern greats in a world-class art institution. (p67)

Schloss Nymphenburg The Schönheitengalerie is one of Munich's most intriguing art spectacles. (p120)

Best Contemporary Art

Haus der Kunst Travelling contemporary shows in a gallery built by the Nazis. (p90)

Museum Brandhorst Southern Germany's top contemporary arts space. (p65)

Museums

There are over 80 museums in Munich, from obscure institutions dedicated to subjects such as the humble potato and hunting to world-famous repositories of the past such as the Deutsches Museum and the Alte Pinakothek. With so much on offer, it pays to be selective.

DOMAGOJ KOVACIC/SHUTTERSTOCK ©

History Museums

Munich's history museums tell the city's story in 3D, from its beginnings as a monkish settlement on the Isar to its postwar rejuvenation.

Art Museums

The capital of Bavaria has long since been regarded a city to be reckoned with when it comes to art history. The Kunstareal and its four globally renowned art museums is unrivalled in the region and there are several other smaller but equally worthwhile museums examining particular areas of art interest.

Transport Museums

You don't have to be in Bavaria long to realise that Germans are slightly obsessed with anything with wheels. This fact is represented in excellent museums crammed with trains, planes and automobiles, the latter usually sporting the badge of the Bayerische Motoren Werke (BMW).

Specialist Museums

Munich has several engaging museums that look at single themes, sometimes of local interest, other times with a wider remit.

FOOTTOO/SHUTTERSTOCK ©

Best History Museums

Jüdisches Museum Learn about the experiences of Munich's Jewish community. (p51)

NS Dokuzentrum Examines the Nazi era in Munich. (p72)

Bayerisches National-museum Delightfully old-fashioned, rambling 19th-century museum. (p89)

Residenz Home to the Wittelsbach ruling family for 500 years. (p40)

Münchner Stadtmuseum The A–Z of Munich's long history. (p44)

Best Art Museums

Kunstareal One parkland, four museums and tens of thousands of exhibits. (p64)

Lenbachhaus Art museum displaying works of Munich's modernist Blue Rider group. (p73)

Glyptothek Sculpture from the ancient world. (p75)

Museum Villa Stuck One of the finest *Jugenstil* villas in Europe. (p109)

Best Transport Museums

Deutsches Museum Vehicles as well as all things technical on an island in the River Isar. (p104)

BMW Museum Showcases the company's cars through the ages. (p125; pictured above left)

Best Specialist Museums

Bier & Oktoberfestmuseum If you can't make it to the fest, this museum will fill you in. (p52)

Museum Reich der Kristalle Museum specialising in precious stones. (p76)

Museum Fünf Kontinente Munich's ethnological museum. (p109; pictured above right)

Museum Mensch und Natur Humankind and nature museum at Schloss Nymphenburg. (p132)

Architecture

It may not have the Gothic splendour of Prague or the high-rise skyline of Manhattan, but what Munich does have is a fascinating architectural story all of its own. With 15th-century churches, ultra-modern stadiums, medieval gates and Jugendstil villas, the city is a mixed bag of stone, brick and glass. Some of the grandest buildings have been commissioned by Munich's rulers, including medieval dukes and Adolf Hitler.

ROLF G WACKENBERG/SHUTTERSTOCK ©

Gothic & Renaissance

There are plenty of broken Gothic arches in Munich, though there's also a fair amount of neo-Gothic faking it. Munich also has some of the finest examples of Renaissance architecture in Germany, since the style spread from Italy to southern Germany before its influence was carried further north.

Baroque & Rococo

As in most of central Europe, the domi-nating architectural styles of the 17th and 18th centuries were the baroque and its short-lived little brother rococo. The superstar duo of the counter-Reformation in Bavaria were the Asam brothers, Cosmas Damian and Egid Quirin.

19th Century

No period in Munich's architectural timeline had as profound an effect on the city's appearance as the 19th century. Down came the stifling city walls, allowing Munich to burst out in a confident march of neo-styles unrivalled in central Europe.

Modern Era

Munich sports a wonderful array of edifices, including examples of *Jugendstil* and buildings from the Fascist era and the 1972 Olympics. Interestingly, there are no high-rise buildings in the old centre as no structure may outdo the 99m of the Frauenkirche's spires.

G215/SHUTTERSTOCK ©

Best Gothic & Renaissance

Hofgarten Munich's sole Renaissance garden. (p53; pictured above left)

Michaelskirche Largest Renaissance church north of the Alps. (p50)

Frauenkirche This church's onion domes are a symbol of the city. (p50)

Best Baroque & Rococo

Cuvilliés Theatre Rococo stage adjoining the Residenz. (p41)

Asamkirche Munich's finest baroque interior. (p50; pictured above right)

Schloss Nymphenburg Exquisite baroque palace in the suburbs. (p120)

Best 19th Century

Königsplatz Leo von Klenze's Greek-revivalist square. (p72)

Maximilianeum The Bavarian parliament building. (p112)

Neues Rathaus The dominant edifice on the central Marienplatz. (p43)

Best Modern Era

Haus der Kunst Built by Hitler to display Nazi-approved art. (p90)

Villa Stuck A fine piece of art nouveau styling. (p109)

Olympiastadion Space age architecture created for the 1972 Olympics. (p123)

BMW Welt Dramatic statement architecture by the car manufacturer. (p125)

Allianz Arena Munich's chameleon-like football stadium – its walls change colour according to which teams are playing. (p73)

For Kids

(Tiny) hands down, Munich is a great city for children, with plenty of activities to please tots with even the shortest attention span. Away from the classic sights there are plenty of parks for romping around, swimming pools and lakes for cooling off, and family-friendly beer gardens with children's playgrounds for making new friends.

Places to Eat

Munich's restaurants are pretty cool about children, though menus specifically for kids are rare. Children are allowed into pubs and beer gardens, the latter are particularly tot-friendly as many have playgrounds.

Green Spaces

There's nothing easier when on holiday than allowing the children to let off steam on a bit of local grass. Munich city centre is well-endowed with green spaces with not a car in sight.

Museums for Kids

Several museums will be of huge interest to inquisitive minds and almost all cater for young ones in some way. Many museums in Munich offer free admission for those aged under 18 years.

Entertainment for Kids

There are lots of ways to keep those minds off screens, with theatre, sea creatures, Bundesliga (the German football league) and cars to check out.

FUTURISTMAN/SHUTTERSTOCK ©

Best Places to Eat with Kids

Schmalznudel Treat the kids to some traditional Munich doughnuts. (p53)

Pommes Boutique All kids like chips and something to dip them in. (p92)

Eiscafé Sarcletti Eyes will light up at the sight of the gelato at Sarcletti's. (p134)

Best Green Spaces

Englischer Garten Hectares of grass for ball and frisbee fun. (p84)

Olympiapark Verdant lawns for picnics and rolling about. (p122)

Best Museums for Kids

Paläontologisches Museum For kids going through their dinosaur phase. (p75)

Deutsches Museum The Kinderreich is arguable the city's top kiddie attraction. (p104)

Museum Mensch und Natur Intriguing displays to stimulate young minds. (p132)

Best Entertainment for Kids

Münchner Theater für Kinder Good, even if they don't speak German. (p78)

Allianz Arena Tours for football-mad offspring. (p73)

Sea Life Budding marine biologists will enjoy this one. (p132)

BMW Hopefully the only time a six-year-old will be allowed behind the wheel of an X6. (p124)

Under the Radar

Despite Munich's popularity among international tourists, there are many corners of the city that remain delightfully offbeat. Wonderfully undiscovered squares, cafes frozen in time and cuisines you'll hardly find anywhere else in Europe complement the Bavarian capital's more mainstream offerings.

STREETFLASH/SHUTTERSTOCK ©

Wiener Platz

Wiener Platz (p107; pictured) – which once marked the start of the road to Vienna – hosts a busy daily gourmet market under a super-size maypole, and has done since 1901. With tiny cafes and kiosks selling everything from fish mains to chocolate to sausages, it's the perfect spot to lunch or snack between sightseeing stops.

Flohmarkt Olympiapark

German cities sure do love a flea market! This intriguing jumble sale (p127) takes place near the Olympiastadion almost every Friday and Saturday from 7am until around 4pm. It provides a superb opportunity to pick up authentic and rather unique retro souvenirs.

Go Afghan

Munich has one of the largest Afghan minorities in Europe, many of its members having been in the city for decades. If you love to try new cuisines, and haven't yet had the opportunity to go Afghan, try Chopan (p134), **Kabul** (Maxvorstadt; www. kabul-kueche.de) and **Lemar** (Altstadt; www. lemar-restaurant.de). Menus are light with rice, dried fruit, grilled meats and salad; but you'll usually search in vain for any alcoholic beverages.

Cafe Jasmin

It's as if the last 40 years never happened at swish Cafe Jasmin (p69) in the Maxvorstadt district. The retro decor here is the real thing and takes you back to the heady days of the *Wirtschaftswunder*.

Tours

Myriad tours now leave Munich Marienplatz on foot, bike and segway to explore every aspect of the city's past and present. There are free walking tours of the Altstadt, trips out to Dachau, beer-themed crawls and specialist tours focusing on subjects such as street art and birdwatching. Booking ahead is always advised, especially in summer.

BY VALET/SHUTTERSTOCK ©

Street Art Tour
(☏ 089-4613 9401; www.streetarttour.org) Operated by an agency called Positive Propaganda, these fascinating street-art tours will show you a completely different side to Munich.

Radius Tours & Bike Rental
Top bike rental and tour company based at the Hauptbahnhof. (p147)

Mike's Bike Tours
(☏ 089-2554 3987; www.mikesbiketours.com; Bräuhausstrasse 10; classic tour €29; S Marienplatz, U Marienplatz) This outfit runs various guided bike tours of the city as well as a couple of other themed excursions.

Segway Tour Munich
(STM; www.seg-tour-munich.com; €75; ☉ tours 8 departures daily; S Marienplatz, U Marienplatz) Three-hour, 12km segway tours led by English speaking guides.

New Europe Munich
(www.neweuropetours.eu; ☉ tours 10am, 10.45am & 2pm; S Marienplatz, U Marienplatz) Departing from Marienplatz, these English-language walking tours tick off all Munich's central landmarks in three hours.

Bus 100 Museenlinie

For a budget tour of Munich's high-brow collections, hop aboard **bus 100 Museenlinie** (www.mvv-muenchen.de), which runs from the Hauptbahnhof to the Ostbahnhof (east station) via 21 of the city's museums and galleries, including all the big hitters. As this is an ordinary bus route, the tour costs no more than a regular public-transport ticket.

Outdoor & Active Munich

VIKTORIIA ADAMCHUK/SHUTTERSTOCK ©

It's easy to get active in Munich, a city that prides itself on its cycling credentials and first-rate sports facilities. There are plenty of parks and gardens for an enjoyable stroll, like the huge Englischer Garten and the Olympiapark. For something less strenuous, why not take a cookery course? Swimming is also a popular pastime here with several pools dotted around the city.

Best Swimming

Müller'sches Volksbad Munich's wonderfully preserved art nouveau swimming pool. (p107)

Olympia Schwimmhalle This well-maintained pool is a legacy of the 1972 Olympics. (p132)

Best Walking

Englischer Garten You can stroll for hours in this huge city park. (p84)

Olympic Park Great for an amble and an urban picnic. (p122)

Best Parks

Englischer Garten The 'green lungs' of the city extend for miles along the River Isar. (p84)

Nymphenburg Grounds Dotted with follies, the grounds of Munich's grandest palace are a joy to wander. (p121)

Olympiapark The rolling lawns here are a venue for many open-air festivals in the warmer months. (p122)

Kunstareal The parkland surrounding the art museums is a good place to lounge between visits. (p64)

Best Gardens

Hofgarten Renaissance gardens with the Dianatempel in the centre. (p53)

Alter Botanischer Garten Former botanical gardens just outside the Altstadt. (p73)

Neuer Botanischer Garten Lush gardens near Schloss Nymphenburg. (p133)

Best Open Spaces

Theresienwiese Better known as Wies'n, this is one of the largest open spaces in Munich, and the site of the Oktoberfest. (p140)

Best for Something Different

Olympia-Eissportzentrum Don skates for a spin round this Olympic rink (p132)

Eisbach Surfing Squeeze yourself into a wetsuit to surf on this wave – or perhaps just watch. (p89; pictured)

Wirtshaus in der Au Cookery Course Learn just how those Bavarian dumplings are made. (p111)

For Free

Munich can be an expensive city but there's plenty to do that won't cost you a euro. None of Munich's churches charge admission and most parks can be roamed for free. A lot of the city's architecture can be admired from street level and even a couple of attractions let you in for nothing, most notably BMW World.

Best Free Churches

Asamkirche No admission is charged to see the city's best baroque interior. (p50)

Michaelskirche You can enter the church for nothing but you'll have to pay to see the crypt. (p50)

Best Free Gardens & Outdoor Spaces

Hofgarten This wonderful Renaissance garden has no ticket office. (p53)

Englischer Garten One of the city's biggest attractions won't cost you anything. (p84; pictured)

Königsplatz Admire the Greek revivalist architecture on this grand square. (p72)

Marienplatz Soak up the atmosphere here. (p42)

Olympiapark Many of the outdoor attractions can be seen without opening your wallet. (p122)

Surfing in the Eisbach It's free to surf, and it's free to watch. (p89)

Best Free Beer Culture

Hofbräuhaus You can wander this huge beer hall at will. (p59)

Oktoberfest There's actually no admission fee to enter the Theresienwiese during Oktoberfest and many attractions and events cost nothing. (p138)

Best Free Museums

Kunstareal OK, it costs a euro on Sundays but that's almost free. (p64)

Paläontologisches Museum One of very few free museums. (p75)

DenkStätte Weisse Rose It's free to view this small exhibition at the university. (p90)

BMW World A top Munich attraction and completely free to get in. (p124)

Best Window Shopping

Viktualienmarkt The market is free to wander, as long as you don't buy anything. (p43)

Four Perfect Days

Day 1

You can easily spend the entire morning exploring Munich's top attraction, the **Residenz** (p40), including the **Cuvilliés-Theater** (p41).

Take the time to peruse the Altstadt starting at the **Marienplatz** (p42). Climb the **St Peterskirche tower** (p43), explore the colourful bounty at the **Viktualienmarkt** (p43; pictured above), then gain insights into the city's evolution at the **Münchner Stadtmuseum** (p44).

End the day at a beer garden. You can gather around a Chinese pagoda folly at the **Chinesischer Turm** (p95) or watch the kids frolic in a playground at the large and leafy **Hirschau** (p97), both of which are in the **Englischer Garten** (p84).

Day 2

Start the day, if you dare, with a breakfast of *Weisswurst* and *Weissbier* (wheat beer) at **Weisses Brauhaus** (p56), which specialises in both. Suitably fortified, head east to the **Englischer Garten** (p84) where a long stroll through the park should burn off those calories.

Spend the afternoon exploring **Schwabing** (p83) – the north of the neighbourhood is resplendent in *Jugendstil* villas, once the haunt of artists and writers. The south, officially **Maxvorstadt** (p63), buzzes with student life, bars, international eateries, vintage-clothes shops and bookstores.

Finish off with a bar hop around the **Gärtnerplatzviertel**, home to some of the most happening cafes and venues.

Day 3

APROTT/GETTY IMAGES ©

You've had the beer, now it's time for Munich's art and a day in the **Kunstareal** (p64), the city's arts quarter — it boasts four major galleries that could each take up half a day. Morning people should use their energy on the **Alte Pinakothek** (p65).

After lunch spend a lazier afternoon in the **Pinakothek der Moderne** (p67) or the **Museum Brandhorst** (p65; pictured above). Alternatively, head to the nearby **Königsplatz** (p72) to admire Greek revivalist architecture from the reign of Ludwig I.

Well, that's the art done, so back to the beer and that quintessential Munich experience, the **Hofbräuhaus beer hall** (p59).

Day 4

YURI ANDREICHYN/SHUTTERSTOCK ©

Leave old Munich for more modern attractions and the city's finest palace. Start off at the **Olympiapark** (p122; pictured above), where you can easily fill the morning exploring the venue of the 1972 Olympic Games.

Post-lunch, pick up the pace with a dash around **BMW Welt** (p125), which has all the latest car models on show, heaps of info about BMW's cars plus various tours and demonstrations. Car enthusiasts might also want to check out the **BMW plant tour** (p130) and **BMW Museum** (p125), but otherwise head to **Schloss Nymphenburg** (p120) for a bit of royal splendour.

End the day kicking back at the **Hirschgarten** (p136), Bavaria's biggest beer garden, along with up to 7999 other drinkers.

Need to Know

For detailed information, see Survival Guide p143

Currency
Euro (€)

Language
German, Bavarian

Visas
Not needed by most nationals for visits of up to 90 days. Check with your local German embassy if unsure.

Money
ATMs are widely available and credit/ debit cards are accepted at most restaurants and hotels. Carry some cash for smaller purchases, ticket machines etc.

Mobile Phones
Germany uses GSM 900, compatible with mobile phones from the rest of Europe, Australia and New Zealand, but not with most North American phones.

Time
Central European Time (GMT plus one hour)

Daily Budget

Budget: Less than €100
Dorm beds: €15–30

Meal: up to €12

Visit museums and galleries on Sundays: many charge €1 admission

Midrange: €100–200
Double room in midrange hotel: €80–160

Three-course dinner at nice restaurant: €30–40

Museum/gallery ticket: €7

Mass of beer (1L) in a pub or beer garden: €8

Top End: More than €200
Luxury hotel room: from €160

Lunch or dinner at top-rated restaurant: €100

Concert or opera tickets: €50–150

Advance Planning

Three months before Make sure you have booked accommodation, especially over the summer. If you want to see a Bayern Munich football match, you'd better get online around now as tickets sell out fast.

One month before Book tickets online to attractions such as the BMW plant tour or the Allianz Arena tour.

One week before Book walking and other city tours online.

Arriving in Munich

Taxis are plentiful at both the airport and the main train station.

✈ Munich Airport

Linked by S-Bahn (S1 and S8) to the Hauptbahnhof - runs every 20 minutes almost 24 hours a day. The Lufthansa Airport Bus shuttles run at 20-minute intervals between the airport and the Hauptbahnhof.

🚉 Hauptbahnhof

Munich's huge main station is well served by trams, buses, the U-Bahn and the S-bahn, which all pass in front of or below the terminus.

Getting Around

Munich's public transport system is affordable and one of central Europe's best. The system is operated by MVV (www.mvv-muenchen.de). Walking is the best way to get around the historical centre.

S Train (S-Bahn)

The S-Bahn reaches out into the suburbs and beyond to satellite towns such as Erding and Dachau almost 24 hours a day. All S-Bahn trains pass through central Munich.

U Subway (U-Bahn)

Munich's extensive U-Bahn runs from the suburbs to the city centre. It's the best way to reach the Olympiapark and the Theresienwiese.

🚋 Tram

Munich's trams link the suburbs with the centre but are slower than the U-Bahn or S-Bahn. They run from around 5am until midnight.

GRAFISSIMO/GETTY IMAGES ©

Munich Neighbourhoods

Nymphenburg, BMW & Olympiapark (p119)

This huge area has two obvious clusters of sights: the Olympiapark/BMW attractions and Schloss Nymphenburg.

Schloss Nymphenburg
◉

Maxvorstadt (p63)

This bustling district has a big focus on art, museums and grand facades, most of which are part of the Kunstareal, Munich's arts quarter.

Schwabing & the Englischer Garten (p83)

Aimless wandering here leads to student hangouts, hip cafes and *Jugendstil* villas, plus the green of the Englischer Garten.

BMW in Munich

Olympiapark

Kunstareal

Englischer Garten

Residenz

Marienplatz

Münchner Stadtmuseum

Deutsches Museum

Oktoberfest

Haidhausen & Lehel (p103)

Trendy residential neighbourhoods where you can visit museums, explore an art nouveau house and stroll the leafy banks of the Isar.

Altstadt & the Residenz (p39)

The Altstadt is Munich's epicentre and it's where you'll find some of the city's best sights, including the Residenz.

Explore
Munich

Neues Rathaus (p43), Marienplatz ROCKY89/GETTY IMAGES ©

Explore ✦

Altstadt & the Residenz

The Altstadt is a must-see for all visitors to Munich – some of the city's best sights, eateries and shops can be found within the inner ring road, at the centre of which is the Marienplatz, the city's main square and an ideal spot to get your bearings.

The nearby Residenz, a sprawling palace from where Bavaria's royals once ruled, should be top of your 'to-visit' list. Combine a trip to the palace with a stroll along Maximilianstrasse, Munich's most exclusive shopping street. In the afternoon visit the Stadtmuseum for the lowdown on the city's history then wander down to the Asamkirche, which offers Munich's finest church interior. Follow this with a spot of shopping in Kaufingerstrasse or at the Stachus before dining at one of the Altstadt's many traditional taverns, such as the inimitable Hofbräuhaus.

Getting There & Around

Ⓤ The main U-Bahn station for the Altstadt is Marienplatz, which is linked to every other part of the city. Karlsplatz (Stachus) is a useful stop for the west of the Altstadt, and Sendlinger Tor for the south.

🚆 Isartor, Marienplatz and Karlsplatz are on the Stammstrecke, the line along which all trains run through central Munich.

Neighbourhood Map on p48

Frauenkirche (p50) WESTEND61/GETTY IMAGES ©

Top Experience 📷

Tour the Wittelsbach Rulers' Spectacular Residenz

Home to Bavaria's all-powerful Wittelsbach rulers from 1508 until WWI, the Residenz is Munich's number one attraction. Taking up a large chunk of the city centre, the Residenz is adjoined by several other quintessential Munich sights. The palace's amazing treasures are on display at the Residenzmuseum, which occupies around half of the Residenz.

◎ MAP P48, E2

www.residenz-muenchen.de

Max-Joseph-Platz 3

adult/concession/under 18yr
€7/6/free

🕙 9am-6pm Apr–mid-Oct, 10am-5pm mid-Oct–Mar, last entry 1hr before closing

Ⓤ Odeonsplatz

The Tour

Tours start at the **Grottenhof**, home of the wonderful **Perseusbrunnen** (Perseus Fountain). Next door is the famous Renaissance **Antiquarium**, a barrel-vaulted hall smothered in frescoes and built to house the Wittelsbachs' antique collection.

Further along the tour route, the neo-Byzantine **Hofkirche** was constructed for Ludwig I in 1826. After WWII only the red-brick walls were left.

Upstairs are the **Kurfürstenzimmer** (Electors Rooms), with some stunning Italian portraits and a passage lined with two-dozen views of Italy, painted by local Romantic artist Carl Rottmann. François Cuvilliés' **Reiche Zimmer** (Rich Rooms), a six-room extravaganza of exuberant rococo decorated by the top stucco and fresco artists of the day, are a definite highlight. More rococo magic awaits in the **Ahnengallery** (Ancestors Gallery), with 121 chronologically-arranged portraits of Bavaria's rulers.

The exquisite **Reichekapelle**, with its blue and gilt ceiling, inlaid marble and 16th-century organ, is considered the finest rococo interior in Bavaria. Another spot to linger is the **Stein zimmer** (Stone Rooms), the emperor's quarters, awash in intricately patterned marble.

Cuvilliés-Theater

Commissioned by Maximilian III in the mid-18th century, François Cuvilliés fashioned one of Europe's finest rococo **theatres** (Residenzstrasse 1; adult/concession/under 18yr €3.50/2.50/free; 2-6pm Mon-Sat, 9am-6pm Sun Apr-Jul & Sep–mid-Oct, 9am-6pm daily Aug, 2-5pm Mon-Sat, 10am-5pm Sun Nov-Mar; Nationaltheater), famous for hosting the premiere of Mozart's opera Idomeneo. Access is limited to the auditorium, where you can take a seat and admire the four tiers of loggia (galleries), dripping with rococo embellishment, at your leisure.

★ Top Tips

o Renovation work is ongoing, closures are inevitable and you may not see all the highlights.

o Arrive early in the day in the summer months to avoid the crowds.

o Admission is free for children aged under 18 years.

o Over winter, the Cuvilliés-Theater is only open in the afternoons.

✕ Take a Break

The world-famous Hofbräuhaus (p59) is just a couple of blocks away.

Cafe Luitpold (p56) is good for a light lunch.

Top Experience 📸

Watch the Glockenspiel on Marienplatz

The epicentral heart and soul of the Altstadt, and indeed of all Munich, Marienplatz is essential viewing for any visitor. It's a popular gathering spot and Munich's busiest piazza by far, with throngs of tourists swarming across its expanse from early morning until late at night. Most walking tours kick off here and several interesting sights cluster around it. In December it's the scene of a vibrant Christmas market.

◉ MAP P48, D4

S Marienplatz,

U Marienplatz

Neues Rathaus

Completely dominating the square's north-ern flank, the soot-blackened façade of the neo-Gothic Neues Rathaus (New Town Hall) is festooned with gargoyles, statues and a turret-scaling dragon; the city's main tourist office is on the ground floor. For pinpointing Munich's landmarks without losing your breath, climb the 85m-tall **tower** (adult/child €3/1; ⏰10am-7pm daily May-Sep, to 5pm Mon-Fri Oct-Apr). Back on the ground look up to watch the **Glockenspiel** (⏰11am, noon, 5pm & 9pm) with its 43 bells and 32 figures that perform two historical events. The top half tells the story of a tournament held in 1568 to celebrate the marriage of Duke Wilhelm V to Renata of Lothringen, while the bottom half portrays the Schäfflertanz (cooper's dance).

Altes Rathaus

On the Marienplatz' eastern flank you'll find the Altes Rathaus (Old Town Hall). Lightning got the better of the medieval original in 1460 and WWII bombs levelled its successor, so what you see is really the third incarnation of the building designed by Jörg von Halspach of Frauenkirche fame. On 9 November 1938 Joseph Goebbels gave a hate-filled speech here that launched the nationwide Kristallnacht pogroms.

St Peterskirche

Just off the southern side of the Marienplatz rises the impressive 1150 **St Peterskirche** (Church of St Peter; Rindermarkt 1; church free, tower adult/child €3/2; ⏰tower 9am-6pm Mon-Fri, from 10am Sat & Sun), central Munich's oldest place of worship. The highlight here is the tower – some 306 steps will take you to the best view of cen-tral Munich. Worth a look inside are the Gothic St-Martin-Altar, the baroque ceiling fresco by Johann Baptist Zimmermann and rococo sculptures by Ignaz Günther.

★ Top Tips

o Don't worry about tired legs when climbing the Neues Rathaus tower – there's a lift.

o The Glockenspiel springs into action every day at 11am and noon, as well as at 5pm March to October.

o Adjoining the Marienplatz is another large square, the Viktualienmarkt with its market and beer garden.

✕ Take a Break

Head to the **Viktualienmarkt** (⏰Mon-Fri & morn-ing Sat) for some top-quality picnic supplies.

The nearby Weisses Brauhaus (p56) is good for a *Weiss-wurst* breakfast until noon or just a snack.

Top Experience 📷

Learn All about the City at Münchner Stadtmuseum

Installed for the city's 850th birthday in 2008, the Münchner Stadtmuseum's Typisch München (Typically Munich) exhibition tells Munich's story in an imaginative, uncluttered and engaging way. Exhibits in each section represent something quintessential about the city. A separate hall gives an excellent and honest account of the city's role in the rise of the Nazis.

◎ MAP P48, C5

www.muenchner-stadt
museum.de

St-Jakobs-Platz 1

adult/concession/child
€7/3.50/free, audioguide free

🕙10am-6pm Tue-Sun

S Marienplatz,
U Marienplatz

Old Munich

Set out in chronological order, the exhibition launches with the founding monks and ends in the postwar-boom decades. The first of five sections, Old Munich, contains a scale model of the city in the late 16th century, but the highlight here is the **The Morris Dancers**, a series of statuettes gyrating like 15th-century ravers. It's one of the most valuable works owned by the city.

New Munich

Next comes New Munich, which charts the city's 18th- and 19th-century transformation into a prestigious royal capital. The **Canaletto View** gives an idea in oil paint of how Munich looked in the mid-18th century, before the Wittelsbachs launched their makeover. The section also takes a fascinating look at the origins of **Oktoberfest** and Munich's cuisine, as well as the phenomenon of the '**Munich Beauty**' – Munich's womenfolk are regarded as Germany's most attractive.

City of Munich & Revue

City of Munich examines the weird and wonderful late-19th and early 20th century, a period known for *Jugenstil* architecture and design, Richard Wagner and avant-garde rumblings in Schwabing. Munich became the 'city of art and beer', a title many are likely to agree it still holds today. The fourth hall, Revue, becomes a little obscure, but basically deals with the aftermath of WWI and the rise of the Nazis.

Nazionalsozialismus in München

The rise of the Nazis has been rightly left as a powerful separate exhibition called Nationalsozialismus in München. Period artefacts and documents charting the early days of the Nazi party occupy an eerily windowless annexe.

★ Top Tips

o Admission is free for children aged under 18 years.

o The museum hosts some top-quality temporary exhibitions, which are included in the ticket price.

o Every second Wednesday of the month the museum is open until 8pm.

✗ Take a Break

Schmalznudel (p53) is a great place for a coffee and pastry halt.

For a light lunch head to vegetarian restaurant Prinz Myshkin (p54).

Walking Tour 🚶

Munich Alstadt Walking Tour

They don't call Munich the 'city of art and beer' for nothing, and once you've seen the art, it's time for the beer. The Bavarian capital has hundreds of places where you can enjoy a dewy 1L Mass, but the Altstadt has a particularly high concentration. Between brews, learn more about the city's unsurpassed brewing traditions at two superb museums.

Walk Facts

Start Augustiner-Gross-gaststätte; Ⓤ Marienplatz

End Hofbräuhaus; Ⓤ Marienplatz

Length 2km, 1 hour

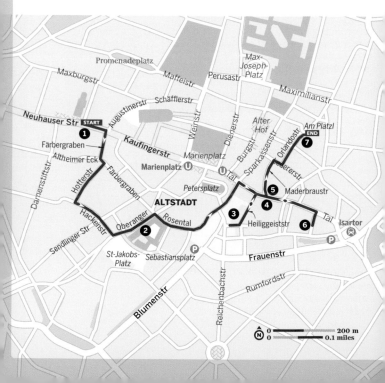

❶ Augustiner-Grossgaststätte

Right in the thick of the retail frenzy on Neuhauser Strasse, this humungous beer temple (p58) belonging to the Augustiner Brewery is as good a place as any to kick off a beer-themed tour of the Altstadt. Out back is a true oasis of peace in the form of an ancient arcaded beer garden complete with flower boxes and murals.

❷ Münchner Stadtmuseum

Among many other themes, the Münchner Stadtmuseum (p44) examines the role of beer and brewing in the city, and the boozy relationship between famous artists and the local suds.

❸ Viktualienmarkt

Munich's most central **beer garden** (Viktualienmarkt 6; ☺9am-10pm; Ⓤ Marienplatz, Ⓢ Marienplatz) is this centuries-old, chestnut-shaded patch among the stalls of the aromatic Viktualienmarkt. Staff in traditional garb offer every kind of Munich beer (though not necessarily at the same time), and there's lots of traditional food to help the froth on its way.

❹ Tegernseer Tal

Time for a little variety at this pleasantly tranquil beer hall (p55) where an intruder from the Alps has the audacity to serve suds to all-comers. Brewed by the crystal waters of the Tegernsee south of Munich, it's one of the few beers from outside the capital that the drinking folk of München will tolerate.

❺ Weisses Brauhaus

Almost opposite the Tegernseer Tal, the Weisses Brauhaus (p56) is one of Munich's most staunchly conservative beer halls, serving its very own wheat beer and the city's finest *Weisswurst* breakfast. In the evening the atmosphere here can be one of the best.

❻ Bier & Oktoberfestmuseum

This must-see museum (p52) for disciples of the hop examines Munich's beer traditions from the Middle Ages onwards, plus the whole Oktoberfest thing. It also holds tasting sessions led by the in-house beer sommelier, and there's a pub where you can apply your freshly acquired theoretical knowledge in a practical way.

❼ Hofbräuhaus

Saving the biggest – and for some the best – till last... Welcome to the mothership of all the world's beer halls, the Hofbräuhaus (p59), with its thousands of carved pine seats, industrial catering operation and raucous oompah-band performances!

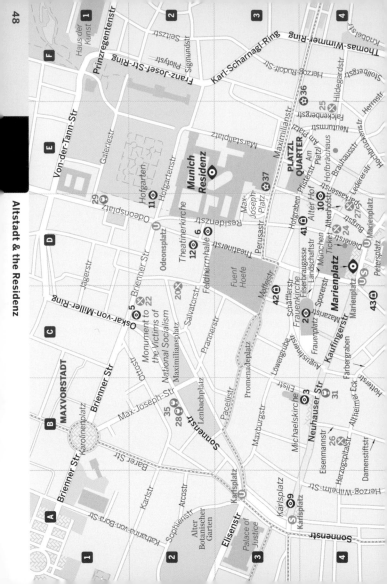

Altstadt & the Residenz

MAXVORSTADT

PLATZL QUARTER

Munich Residenz

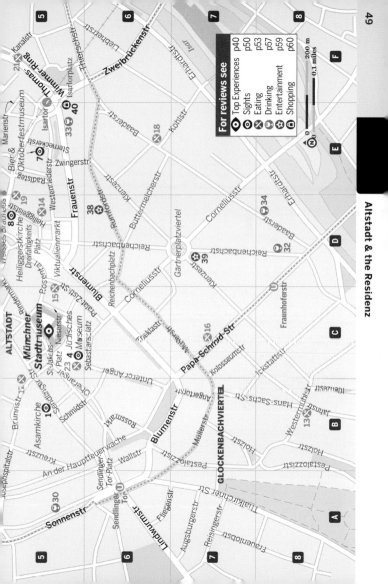

Altstadt & the Residenz

For reviews see

● Top Experiences	p40
● Sights	p50
✕ Eating	p53
✕ Drinking	p57
✿ Entertainment	p59
● Shopping	p60

0   200 m
0   0.1 miles

ALTSTADT

Münchner Stadtmuseum

GLOCKENBACHVIERTEL

Sights

Asamkirche   CHURCH

1 MAP P48, B5

Though pocket sized, the late-baroque Asamkirche, constructed in 1746, is as rich and epic as a giant's treasure chest. Its creators, the brothers Cosmas Damian Asam and Egid Quirin Asam (p97), dug deep into their considerable repertoire of talent to swathe every inch of the wall space with gilt garlands and docile cherubs, false marble and oversized barley-twist columns. See more of the Asam brothers' designs in the Heiliggeist-kirche (p52).(Sendlinger Strasse 32; ⏰9am-6pm; 🚋Sendlinger Tor, Ⓤ Sendlinger Tor)

Frauenkirche   CHURCH

2 MAP P48, C4

The landmark Frauenkirche, built between 1468 and 1488, is Munich's spiritual heart and the Mt Everest among its churches. No other building in the central city may stand taller than its onion-domed twin towers, which reach a skyscraping 99m. The south tower can be climbed, but has been under urgent renovation for several years. (Church of Our Lady; www.muenchner-dom.de; Frauenplatz 1; ⏰7.30am-8.30pm; Ⓢ Marienplatz)

Michaelskirche   CHURCH

3 MAP P48, B4

It stands quiet and dignified amid the retail frenzy out on Kaufinger-strasse, but to fans of Ludwig II,

Feldherrnhalle

MIKHAIL MARKOVSKIY/SHUTTERSTOCK ©

Top Five Views of Munich

Here are our top five places from which to get a bird's-eye view of the Bavarian capital:

Bavariastatue (p140) See the Oktoberfest through the statue's eyes.

Frauenkirche Put the Alps and Altstadt at your feet.

Monopteros (p90) Survey the charms of the English Garden.

Olympiaturm (p123) Ogle panoramic views of up to 100km.

St Peterskirche (p43) Survey all of Munich's major landmarks.

the Michaelskirche is the ultimate place of pilgrimage. Its dank crypt is the final resting place of the Mad King, whose humble tomb is usually drowned in flowers. (Church of St Michael; www.st-michael-muenchen.de; Kaufingerstrasse 52; crypt €2; ⊙crypt 9.30am-4.30pm Mon-Fri, to 2.30pm Sat & Sun; Karlsplatz, Karlsplatz, Karlsplatz)

Jüdisches Museum   MUSEUM

4 ⊙ MAP P48, C5

Coming to terms with its Nazi past has not historically been a priority in Munich, which is why the opening of the Jewish Museum in 2007 was hailed as a milestone. The permanent exhibition offers an insight into Jewish history, life and culture in the city. The Holocaust is dealt with, but the focus is clearly on contemporary Jewish culture. (Jewish Museum; www.juedisches-museum-muenchen.de; St-Jakobs-Platz 16; adult/child €6/3; ⊙10am-6pm Tue-Sun; Sendlinger Tor, Sendlinger Tor)

Monument to the Victims of National Socialism   MONUMENT

5 ⊙ MAP P48, C2

This striking monument is made up of four Ts holding up a block-like cage in which an eternal flame gutters in remembrance of those who died at the hands of the Nazis due to their political beliefs, race, religion, sexual orientation or disability. Moved to this spot in 2014, it's a sternly simple reminder of Munich's not-so-distant past. (Brienner Strasse; Odeonsplatz)

Feldherrnhalle   HISTORIC BUILDING

6 ⊙ MAP P48, D2

Corking up Odeonsplatz' southern side is Friedrich von Gärnter's Feldherrnhalle, modelled on the Loggia dei Lanzi in Florence. The structure pays homage to the Bavarian army and positively drips with testosterone; check out the statues of General Johann Tilly, who kicked the Swedes out of Munich during

Bayerisches Staatsschauspiel

This leading **ensemble** (☏089-2185 1940; www.residenztheater.de) has gone alternative in recent years, staging Shakespeare, Schiller and other tried-and-true playwrights in 21st-century garb and the like. Performances are in the **Residenztheater** (☏089-2185 1940; www.residenztheater.de; Max-Joseph-Platz 2; ☒Nationaltheater), the **Theater im Marstall** (☏089-2185 1940; www.residenztheater.de; Marstallplatz 4; ☒Kammerspiele) and the Cuvilliés-Theater (p41).

the Thirty Years' War; and Karl Philipp von Wrede, an ally turned foe of Napoleon. (Field Marshalls Hall; Residenzstrasse 1; Ⓤ Odeonsplatz)

Bier & Oktoberfestmuseum MUSEUM

7 ◉ MAP P48, E5

Head to this popular museum to learn all about Bavarian suds and the world's most famous booze-up. The four floors heave with old brewing vats, historic photos and some of the earliest Oktoberfest regalia. The 14th-century building has some fine medieval features, including painted ceilings and a kitchen with an open fire. (Beer & Oktoberfest Museum; www.bier-und-oktoberfestmuseum.de; Sterneckerstrasse 2; adult/concession €4/2.50; ⊙1-6pm Tue-Sat; ☒Isartor, Ⓢ Isartor)

Heiliggeistkirche CHURCH

8 ◉ MAP P48, D5

Gothic at its core, this baroque church on the edge of the Viktualienmarkt has fantastic ceiling frescoes created by the Asam brothers in 1720, depicting the foundation of a hospice that once stood next door. The hospice was demolished to make way for the Viktualienmarkt. (Church of the Holy Spirit; Tal 77; ⊙7am-6pm; Ⓢ Marienplatz, Ⓤ Marienplatz)

Karlsplatz SQUARE

9 ◉ MAP P48, A3

Karlsplatz and the medieval Karlstor (a gate) form the western entrance to the Altstadt and the pedestrianised shopping precinct along Neuhauser Strasse and Kaufinger Strasse. The busy square was laid out in 1791 as an ego project of the highly unpopular Elector Karl Theodor. (☒Karlsplatz, Ⓢ Karlsplatz, Ⓤ Karlsplatz)

Alter Hof PALACE

10 ◉ MAP P48, D4

Alter Hof was the starter home of the Wittelsbach family and has its origins in the 12th century. The Bavarian rulers moved out of this central palace as long ago as the 15th century. Visitors can only see the central courtyard, where the bay window on the southern facade was nicknamed Monkey Tower in honour of a valiant ape that saved the infant Ludwig the

Bavarian from the clutches of a ferocious market pig. Local lore at its most bizarre. (Burgstrasse 8; S Marienplatz, U Marienplatz)

Hofgarten
GARDENS

11 MAP P48, D2

Office workers catching some rays during their lunch break, stylish mothers pushing prams, seniors on bikes, a gaggle of chatty nuns – everybody comes to the Hofgarten. The formal court gardens, with fountains, radiant flower beds, lime-tree-lined gravel paths and benches galore, sit just north of the Residenz. Paths converge at the **Dianatempel**, a striking octagonal pavilion honouring the Roman goddess of the hunt. Enter the gardens from Odeonsplatz. (U Odeonsplatz)

Theatinerkirche
CHURCH

12 MAP P48, D2

The mustard-yellow Theatinerkirche, built to commemorate the 1662 birth of Prince Max Emanuel, is the work of Swiss architect Enrico Zuccalli. Also known as St Kajetan's, it's a voluptuous design with massive twin towers flanking a giant cupola. Inside, an ornate dome lords it over the Fürstengruft (royal crypt), the final destination of several Wittelsbach rulers, including King Maximilian II (1811–64). (Theatinerstrasse 22; admission free; 7am-9pm; S Odeonsplatz)

Eating

Götterspeise
CAFE €

13 MAP P48, B8

The name of this cafe translates as 'food of the gods' and the food in question is that most addictive of treats, chocolate. Here it comes in many forms, both liquid and solid, but there are also teas, coffees and cakes and little outside perches for when the sun shines. (Jahnstrasse 30; snacks from €3.50; 8am-7pm Mon-Fri, to 6pm Sat; Müllerstrasse)

Bratwurstherzl
FRANCONIAN €

14 MAP P48, D5

Cosy panelling and an ancient vaulted brick ceiling set the tone of this Old Munich tavern with a Franconian focus. Homemade organic sausages are grilled to perfection on an open beechwood fire and served on heart-shaped pewter plates. They're best enjoyed with a cold one from the Hacker-Pschorr brewery. (Dreifaltigkeitsplatz 1; mains €7-12; 10am-11pm Mon-Sat; S Marienplatz, U Marienplatz)

Schmalznudel
CAFE €

15 MAP P48, C5

This incredibly popular institution serves just four traditional pastries, one of which, the *Schmalznudel* (an oily type of doughnut), gives the place its local nickname. All baked goodies you munch here are crisp and fragrant, as they're always fresh off the hotplate. They're best eaten with a steaming

Altstadt & the Residenz Eating

pot of coffee on a winter's day. (Cafe Frischhut; Prälat-Zistl-Strasse 8; pastries €2.10; ⊗8am-6pm Mon-Sat; §Marienplatz, ⓊMarienplatz)

Fraunhofer

BAVARIAN €€

16 ✕ MAP P48, C7

With its screechy parquet floors, stuccoed ceilings, wood panelling and virtually no trace that the last century even happened, this wonderfully characterful inn is perfect for exploring the region with a fork. The menu is a seasonally adapted checklist of southern German favourites but also features at least a dozen vegetarian dishes and the odd exotic ingredient. Cash only. (☑089-266 460; www.fraunhofertheater.de; Fraunhoferstrasse 9; mains €5-20; ⊗4.30pm-1am; ☑; 🚊Müllerstrasse)

Prinz Myshkin

VEGETARIAN €€

17 ✕ MAP P48, B5

This place is proof, if any were needed, that the vegetarian experience has well and truly left the sandals, beards and lentils era. Ensconced in a former brewery, Munich's premier meat-free dining spot occupies a gleamingly whitewashed, vaulted space where health-conscious eaters come to savour imaginative dishes such as curry-orange-carrot soup, unexpectedly good curries and 'wellness desserts'. (☑089-265 596; www.prinzmyshkin.com; Hackenstrasse 2; mains €9-20; ⊗11am-12.30am; ☑; §Marienplatz, ⓊMarienplatz)

Marienplatz (p42)

Königsquelle

EUROPEAN €€

18 🍽 MAP P48, E6

This wood-panelled Munich institution is well loved for its attentive service, expertly prepared food and dark, well-stocked hardwood bar containing what must be the Bavarian capital's best selection of malt whiskies, stacked high behind the bar. The only-just decipherable handwritten menu hovers somewhere mid-Alps, with anything from schnitzel to linguine and goat's cheese to cannelloni to choose from. (☎089-220 071; www.koenigsquelle.com; Baaderplatz 2; mains €10-27; ⏱5pm-1am Sun-Fri, from 7pm Sat; 🚇Isartor, 🚋Isartor, 🚈Isartor)

Tegernseer Tal

BAVARIAN €€

19 🍽 MAP P48, D5

A blond-wood interior illuminated by a huge skylight makes this a bright alternative to Munich's dark-panelled taverns. And with Alpine Tegernseer beer on tap and an imaginative menu of regional food, this is generally a lighter, calmer, more refined beer-hall experience with a less raucous ambience. (☎089-222 626; www.tegernseer-tal8.com; Tal 8; mains €10-20; ⏱9.30am-1am Sun-Wed, to 3am Thu-Sat; 🛜; 🚈Marienplatz, 🚇Marienplatz)

OskarMaria

INTERNATIONAL €€

20 🍽 MAP P48, C2

The bookish cafe at the Literaturhaus cultural centre is a

Altstadt Pride

In mid-July the Altstadt plays host to the Christopher Street Day, the biggest gay event in the calendar.

commendably stylish spot, with high ceilings, rows of small central-European cafe tables and sprightly waiters. The more highbrow atmosphere will be appreciated by those who prefer their eateries (virtually) tourist free, and the menu features international staples plus several Bavarian favourites. (www.oskarmaria.com; Salvatorplatz 1; mains €9-23; ⏱10am-midnight Mon-Sat, to 7pm Sun; 🍽; 🚇Odeonsplatz)

Vegelangelo

VEGETARIAN €€

21 🍽 MAP P48, F5

Reservations are compulsory at this petite veggie spot, where Indian odds and ends, a piano and a small Victorian fireplace distract little from the superb meat-free cooking, all of which can be converted to suit vegans. There's a set-menu-only policy Friday and Saturday. No prams allowed and no tap water served, but it does accept Bitcoin. (☎089-2880 6836; www.vegelangelo.de; Thomas-Wimmer-Ring 16; mains €13-19, set menu €22-34; ⏱noon-2pm Tue-Thu, 6pm-late Mon-Sat; 🍽; 🚇Isartor, 🚈Isartor)

Weisswurst Breakfast 🍽

A culinary experience you shouldn't miss is a *Weisswurst* breakfast at the Altstadt's **Weisses Brauhaus** (Map p48, E5; 📞089-290 1380; www.weisses-brauhaus.de; Tal 7; mains €7-20; ⏰8am-12.30am; Ⓢ Marienplatz, Ⓤ Marienplatz). Downing a pair of white veal sausages, a fresh pretzel and a mug of wheat beer at 9am is an essential Munich experience and nowhere does it better. In line with tradition, the tavern only serves *Weisswurst* until noon, after which it is considered stale.

Cafe Luitpold   CAFE €€

24 ✕ MAP P48, C2

A cluster of pillarbox-red streetside tables and chairs announces you've arrived at this stylish but not ubercool retreat. It offers a choice of three spaces: a lively bar, a less boisterous columned cafe, and a cool palm-leaved atrium. Good for a daytime coffee-and-cake halt or a full evening blowout with all the trimmings. (www.cafe-luitpold.de; Briennerstrasse 11; mains €10-19; ⏰8am-7pm Mon, to 11pm Tue-Sat, 9am-7pm Sun; 📶; Ⓤ Odeonsplatz)

Einstein   JEWISH €€

23 ✕ MAP P48, C5

Reflected in the plate-glass windows of the Jewish Museum, this is the only kosher eatery in the city centre. The ID-and-bag-search entry process is worth it for the restaurant's uncluttered lines, smartly laid tables, soothing ambience and menu of well-crafted Jewish dishes. Reservations online only. (📞089-202 400 332; www.einstein-restaurant.de; St-Jakobs-Platz 18; mains €19-20; ⏰noon-3pm & 6pm-midnight Sat-Thu, 12.30-3pm Fri; 📶; Ⓡ Marienplatz, Ⓤ Marienplatz)

Alois Dallmayr   FOOD HALL €€

24 ✕ MAP P48, D4

A pricey gourmet delicatessen right in the thick of the Altstadt action, Alois Dallmayr is best known for its coffee but has so much more, including cheeses, ham, truffles, wine, caviar and exotic foods from every corner of the globe. (📞089-213 50; www.dallmayr.de; Dienerstrasse 14; ⏰9.30am-7pm Mon-Sat; Ⓢ Marienplatz, Ⓤ Marienplatz)

Conviva im Blauen Haus   INTERNATIONAL €€

25 ✕ MAP P48, E4

The industrially exposed interior and barely dressed tables mean nothing distracts from the great food at this theatre restaurant. The daily-changing menus make the most of local seasonal ingredients and are reassuringly short. The lunch menu is a steal. (www.conviva-muenchen.de; Hildegardstrasse 1; 3-course lunch €8-10, dinner mains €10-22; ⏰11am-

1am Mon-Sat, from 5pm Sun; ▄;
🏛Kammerspiele)

Weinhaus Neuner · BAVARIAN €€€

26 ❌ MAP P48, B4

This Munich institution has been
serving Bavarian-Austrian classics and a long wine list for well
over 100 years. Take a break from
the hop-infused frenzy and pork
knuckle to enjoy schnitzel and
Tafelspitz (boiled veal or beef),
helped along with a Franconian Riesling or a Wachau Grüner
Veltiner amid the understated
surroundings of the wood-panelled
dining room. Reservations advised.
(🕿089-260 3954; www.weinhaus-
neuner.de; Herzogspitalstrasse 8;
mains €20-25; 🕙noon-midnight;
Ⓢ Karlsplatz, Ⓤ Karlsplatz)

Galleria · ITALIAN €€€

27 ❌ MAP P48, D4

Munich has a multitude of Italian
eateries, but Galleria is a cut above
the rest. The compact interior hits
you first, a multihued, eclectic mix
of contemporary art and tightly
packed tables. The menu throws
up a few surprises – some dishes
contain very un-Italian ingredients,
such as curry and coconut. Reservations are pretty much essential
in the evening. (🕿089-297 995;
www.ristorante-galleria.de; Sparkassen
strasse 11; mains €17.50-30; 🕙noon-
2.30pm & 6-11pm; Ⓢ Marienplatz,
Ⓤ Marienplatz)

Drinking

Pacha · CLUB

28 🍷 MAP P48, B2

One of a gaggle of clubs at
Maximiliansplatz 5, this nightspot with its cherry logo is one of
Munich's hottest nights out, with
the DJs spinning their stuff till
well after sunrise. (www.pacha-
muenchen.de; Maximiliansplatz 5;
🕙7pm-6am Thu, 11pm-6am Fri & Sat;
🏛Lenbachplatz)

Schumann's Bar · BAR

29 🍷 MAP P48, D1

Urbane and sophisticated,
Schumann's shakes up Munich's
nightlife with libational flights of
fancy and an impressive range
of concoctions. It's also good for
weekday breakfasts. It accepts
cash only. (🕿089-229 060; www.
schumanns.de; Odeonsplatz 6-7;
🕙8am-3am Mon-Fri, 6pm-3am Sat &
Sun; Ⓢ Odeonsplatz)

milchundbar · CLUB

30 🍷 MAP P48, A5

One of the hottest addresses
in the city centre for those who
like to spend the hours between
supper and breakfast boogieing
to an eclectic mix of nostalgia hits
during the week and top DJs at
the weekends. (www.milchundbar.de;
Sonnenstrasse 27; 🕙10pm-7am Mon-
Thu, 11pm-9am Fri & Sat; 🏛Sendlinger
Tor, Ⓤ Sendlinger Tor)

Augustiner-Grossgaststätte

BEER HALL

31 ⊜ MAP P48, B4

This sprawling place has a less raucous atmosphere and superior food to the usual offerings. Altogether it's a much more authentic example of an old-style Munich beer hall, but with the added highlight of a tranquil arcaded beer garden out back. (📞089-2318 3257; www.augustiner-restaurant.com; Neuhauser Strasse 27; ⊙9am-11.30pm)

Trachtenvogl

CAFE

32 ⊜ MAP P48, D8

At night you'll have to shoehorn your way into this buzzy lair favoured by a chatty, boozy crowd of scenesters, artists and students. Daytimes are more mellow – all the better to sample its seasonal menu and check out the incongruous collection of knick-knacks left over from the days when this was a traditional garment shop. (www.trachtenvogl.de; Reichenbachstrasse 47; ⊙9am-10pm; 🛜; 🚊Fraunhoferstrasse)

Braunauer Hof

BEER HALL

33 ⊜ MAP P48, E5

Near the Isartor, drinkers can choose between the traditional Bavarian interior or the beer garden out the back, which enjoys a surprisingly tranquil setting despite its city-centre location. Most come for the Paulaner beer in the evening, but the €8.50 lunch menu

Hofbräuhaus

A Celebrated Beer Hall

Even teetotalling, uber-cool kitsch-haters will at some point gravitate, out of simple curiosity, to the **Hofbräuhaus** (Map p48, E4; ☎089-2901 36100; www.hofbraeuhaus.de; Am Platzl 9; ☺9am-midnight; 🚋Kammerspiele, ⑤Marienplatz, ⓊMarienplatz), the world's most celebrated beer hall. The constant hordes of tourists tend to overshadow the sterling interior, where dainty twirled flowers and Bavarian flags adorn the medieval vaults.

Beer guzzling and pretzel snapping has been going on here since 1644 and the ballroom upstairs was the site of the first large meeting of the National Socialist Party on 20 February 1920.

is commendable value for money. (www.wirtshaus-im-braunauer-hof.de; Frauenstrasse 42; ☺10am-midnight Mon-Sat, to 10pm Sun; 🚋Isartor, ⑤Isartor)

Baader Café   CAFE

34 🍴 MAP P48, D8

Around since the mid-'80s, this literary think-and-drink place lures all sorts, from short skirts to tweed jackets, who linger over daytime coffees and nighttime cocktails. It's normally packed, even on winter Wednesday mornings, and is popular among Brits who come for the authentic English breakfast. (www.baadercafe.de; Baaderstrasse 47; ☺9.30am-1am Sun-Thu, to 2am Fri & Sat; 🛜; 🚋Fraunhoferstrasse)

Rote Sonne   CLUB

35 🍴 MAP P48, B2

Named for a 1969 Munich cult movie starring it-girl Uschi Obermaier, the Red Sun is a fiery nirvana for fans of electronic sounds. A global roster of DJs keeps the dance floor packed and sweaty until the sun rises. (www.rote-sonne.com; Maximiliansplatz 5; ☺from 11pm Thu-Sun; 🚋Lenbachplatz)

Entertainment

Münchner Kammerspiele   THEATRE

36 ⭐ MAP P48, F4

A venerable theatre with an edgy bent, the Kammerspiele delivers provocative interpretations of the classics as well as works by contemporary playwrights. Performances are in a beautifully refurbished art nouveau theatre at Maximilianstrasse 26 and in the **Neues Haus** (Falckenbergstrasse 1; 🚋Kammerspiele), a 21st-century glass cube nearby. (☎089-2339 6600; www.muenchner-kammerspiele.de; Maximilianstrasse 26; 🚋Kammerspiele)

Tickets & Reservations

Tickets to cultural and sporting events are available at venue box offices and official ticket outlets, such as **München Ticket** (Map p48, D4; ☑089-5481 8181; www.muenchenticket.de; Marienplatz; �

 10am-8pm Mon-Sat; Ⓤ Marienplatz, Ⓢ Marienplatz), which shares premises with the tourist office.

Bayerische Staatsoper   OPERA

37 ⭐ MAP P48, E3

One of the world's best opera companies, the Bavarian State Opera performs to sell-out crowds at the **Nationaltheater** (Max-Joseph-Platz 2; 🚋 Nationaltheater) in the Residenz and puts the emphasis on Mozart, Strauss and Wagner. In summer it hosts the prestigious **Opernfestspiele** (Opera Festival; www.muenchner-opernfestspiele.de; ☀Jul). The opera's house band is the **Bayerisches Staatsorchester**, in business since 1523 and thus Munich's oldest orchestra. (Bavarian State Opera; ☑089-2185 1025; www.staatsoper.de)

Jazzbar Vogler   JAZZ

38 ⭐ MAP P48, D6

This intimate watering hole brings some of Munich's baddest cats to the stage. You never know who'll show up for Monday's jam session, and Tuesday to Thursday are live piano nights, but the main acts take to the stage on Friday and Saturday. Cash only. (www.jazzbar-vogler.com; Rumfordstrasse 17; €2-6; ☀7pm-midnight Mon-Thu, to 1am Fri & Sat; 🚋 Reichenbachplatz)

Staatstheater am Gärtnerplatz   PERFORMING ARTS

39 ⭐ MAP P48, D7

Spruced up to southern German standards for its 150th birthday in November 2015, this grand theatre specialises in light opera, musicals and dance. (☑089-2185 1960; www.gaertnerplatztheater.de; Gärtnerplatz 3; 🚋 Reichenbachplatz)

Shopping

Globetrotter   SPORTS & OUTDOORS

40 🅖 MAP P48, E5

Munich's premier outdoors and travel stockist is worth a browse even if you've never pulled on a pair of hiking boots. The basement boasts a lake for testing out kayaks and there's a travel agent and even a branch of the Alpenverein, plus every travel accessory you could ever possibly need. (www.globetrotter.de; Isartorplatz 8-10; ☀10am-8pm Mon-Sat; Ⓤ Isartor, Ⓢ Isartor)

Manufactum   HOMEWARES

41 🅖 MAP P48, D4

Anyone with an admiration for top-quality design from Germany and

Cuvilliés-Theater (p41)

ery. The stock changes according to the season. (www.manufactum.de; Dienerstrasse 12; ⊙9.30am-7pm Mon-Sat; Ⓢ Marienplatz, 🚋 Marienplatz)

Loden-Frey
CLOTHING

42 🔒 MAP P48, C3

The famous cloth producer stocks a wide range of Bavarian wear and other top-end clothes. The Lederhosen and Dirndl outfits are a cut above the discount night-out versions and prices are accordingly high. (📞089-210 390; www.lodenfrey.com; Maffeistrasse 5-7; ⊙10am-8pm Mon-Sat; 🚋Theatinerstrasse)

Schuster
SPORTS & OUTDOORS

43 🔒 MAP P48, C4

Get tooled up for the Alps at this sports megastore with seven floors of equipment, including cycling, skiing, travel and camping gear. (Rosenstrasse 1-5; ⊙10am-8pm Mon-Sat; Ⓢ Marienplatz, Ⓤ Marienplatz)

further afield should make a beeline for this store. Last-a-lifetime household items compete for shelf space with retro toys, Bauhaus lamps and times-gone-by station-

Explore ⬙

Maxvorstadt

'Museums and universities' pretty much sums up Maxvorstadt, meaning most visitors are likely to spend some time here. The Pinakotheken and Brandhorst art museums form the Kunstareal, while the Ludwig-Maximilians-Universität and venerable Kunstakademie (Art Academy) bustle with student activity. The area has been a hotbed of culture since the early 20th century; painters Franz Marc and Wassily Kandinsky had their studios here, and Thomas Mann used to talk literature with colleagues in smoky coffeehouses. Today students shape the neighbourhood vibe.

How you spend a day in Maxvorstadt really depends on your artistic tastes, but whatever your preferences, be prepared to overdose on some of the best art in central Europe: the Kunstareal (p64) with its four world-class art museums is one of Munich's major highlights. Away from the oils and installations, the area around Königsplatz (p72) has a darker story to tell as it was here that Hitler erected the Nazis' admin buildings – the NS Dokuzentrum (p72) tells the tale. End the day in one of the studenty bars.

Getting There & Around

🚌 Bus 100 passes through the Kunstareal on its way from the Hauptbahnhof to the Ostbahnhof. The Pinakotheken have their own dedicated stop.

Ⓤ Königsplatz is served by the U2.

🚋 The Pinakotheken stop is served by tram 27.

Neighbourhood Map on p70

Top Experience 📷

Allow Plenty of Time for the Kunstareal's Museums

Munich's unrivalled Kunstareal is a compact area packed with southern Germany's finest art museums – some of the city's must-sees. The Alte Pinakothek, the Museum Brandhorst, the Neue Pinakothek and the Pinakothek der Moderne will keep art fans busy for at least half a day each – many travel to the Bavarian capital specifically to spend time amid these high-brow institutions.

◉ MAP P70, G3

www.kunstareal.de

🚃 Pinakotheken,
🚃 Pinakotheken

Alte Pinakothek

Munich's main repository of Old European Masters, the **Alte Pinakothek** (📞089-238 0516; www.pinakothek.de; Barer Strasse 27; adult/concession/child €7/5/free, Sun €1, audioguide €4.50; ⊕10am-8pm Tue, to 6pm Wed-Sun) is crammed with all the major players who daubed canvases between the 14th and 18th centuries. This neoclassical temple was masterminded by Leo von Klenze and is a delicacy to be savoured, even if you can't tell your Rembrandt from your Rubens. The collection is world famous for its exceptional quality and depth, especially when it comes to German masters.

A key room is the Dürersaal upstairs. Here hangs Albrecht Dürer's famous Christlike *Self-Portrait* (1500), showing the gaze of an artist brimming with self-confidence. His final major work, *The Four Apostles*, depicts John, Peter, Paul and Mark as rather humble men, in keeping with post-Reformation ideas. Compare this to Matthias Grünewald's *Sts Erasmus and Maurice*, which shows the saints dressed in rich robes like kings.

There's a choice bunch of works by Dutch masters, including an altarpiece by Rogier van der Weyden called *The Adoration of the Magi*, plus *The Seven Joys of Mary* by Hans Memling, *Danae* by Jan Gossaert and *The Land of Cockayne* by Pieter Bruegel the Elder. At 6m in height, Rubens' epic *Last Judgment* is so big that Klenze custom-designed the hall for it. A memorable portrait is *Hélène Fourment* (1631), a youthful beauty who was the ageing Rubens' second wife.

Museum Brandhorst

A big, bold and aptly abstract building, clad entirely in vividly multihued ceramic tubes, the **Brandhorst** (www.museum-brandhorst.de; Theresienstrasse 35a; adult/concession/child €7/5/free, Sun €1; ⊕10am-6pm Tue, Wed & Fri-Sun, to

★ Top Tips

• Inevitably, the €1 admission means Sunday is by far the busiest day – come midweek for a more tranquil experience.

• At the time of research, the Neue Pinakothek was undergoing a much-needed renovation. During this time, part of the collection will be on display at the Alte Pinakothek.

• The Kunstareal Fest takes place in late June featuring tens of themed tours, though most are in German.

✕ Take a Break

The famous Alter Simpl (p77) pub is a superb place for a quick lunch in between museums.

Schall & Rauch (p95) serves light meals as well as coffee and snacks.

8pm Thu; Maxvorstadt/Sammlung Brandhorst, Pinakotheken) jostled its way into the Munich Kunstareal in a punk blaze of colour in 2009. Its walls, its floor and occasionally its ceiling provide space for some of the most challenging art in the city, among it some instantly recognisable 20th-century images by Andy Warhol, whose work dominates the collection.

Pop Art's 1960s poster boy pops up throughout the gallery and even has an entire room dedicated to pieces such as his punkish *Self-Portrait* (1986), *Marilyn* (1962) and *Triple Elvis* (1963).

The other prevailing artist at the Brandhorst is the lesser-known Cy Twombly. His arrestingly spectacular splash-and-dribble canvases are a bit of an acquired taste, but this is the place to acquire it if ever there was one.

Elsewhere Dan Flavin floodlights various corners with his eye-watering light installations and other big names such as Mario Merz, Alex Katz and Sigmar Polke also make an appearance. Damien Hirst gets a look-in here and there.

Neue Pinakothek

The **Neue Pinakothek** (☎089-2380 5195; www.pinakothek.de; Barer Strasse 29; adult/child €7/free, Sun €1; ⏲10am-6pm Thu-Mon, to 8pm Wed; Pinakotheken, Pinakotheken) harbours a well-respected collection of 19th- and early-20th-century paintings and sculpture, from rococo to *Jugendstil* (art nouveau). All the world-famous household names get wall space here, including

Pinakothek der Moderne

crowd-pleasing French impressionists such as Monet, Cézanne and Degas, as well as Van Gogh, whose boldly pigmented *Sunflowers* (1888) radiates cheer.

Perhaps the most memorable canvases, though, are by Romantic painter Caspar David Friedrich, who specialised in emotionally charged, brooding landscapes.

There are also several works by Gauguin, including *Breton Peasant Women* (1894), and Manet, including *Breakfast in the Studio* (1869). Turner gets a look-in with his dramatically sublime *Ostende* (1844).

Local painters represented in the exhibition include Carl Spitzweg and Wilhelm von Kobell of the Dachau School, and Munich society painters such as Wilhelm von Kaulbach, Franz Lenbach and Karl von Piloty. Another focus is work by the Deutschrömer (German Romans), a group of neoclassicists centred on Johann Koch, who stuck mainly to Italian landscapes.

Pinakothek der Moderne

Germany's largest modern-art museum, **Pinakothek der Moderne** (☎089-2380 5360; www.pinakothek. de; Barer Strasse 40; adult/child €10/ free, Sun €1; ☺10am-6pm Tue, Wed & Fri-Sun, to 8pm Thu; ⛪Pinakotheken, ⛪Pinakotheken) unites four significant collections under a single roof: 20th-century art, applied design from the 19th century to today, a graphics collection and an architecture museum. It's housed in a spectacular building by Stephan Braunfels, whose four-storey interior centres on a vast eye-like dome through which soft natural light filters throughout the blanched white galleries.

The State Gallery of Modern Art has some exemplary modern classics by Picasso, Klee, Dalí and Kandinsky and many lesser-known works that will be new to most visitors. More recent big shots include Georg Baselitz, Andy Warhol, Cy Twombly, Dan Flavin and the late enfant terrible Joseph Beuys.

In a world obsessed by retro style, the New Collection is the busiest section of the museum. Housed in the basement, it focuses on applied design from the industrial revolution via art nouveau and Bauhaus to today. VW Beetles, Eames chairs and early Apple Macs stand alongside more obscure interwar items that wouldn't be out of place in a Kraftwerk video. There's lots of 1960s furniture, the latest spool tape recorders and an exhibition of the weirdest jewellery you'll ever see.

Walking Tour 🥾

Off the Beaten Track in Maxvorstadt

Maxvorstadt is all about big-name art and Nazi buildings, right? Well, even this small Munich neighbourhood has a B side, the grid of streets west of the Königsplatz and the Pinakotheken throwing up some wonderfully distinctive but wholly unvisited sights. With its timewarped cafes and impressive church architecture, uncover a part of Munich few except the locals really know.

Walk Facts

Start Alter Botanischer Garten; Ⓤ Karlsplatz

End Nordbard; Ⓤ Hohenzollernplatz

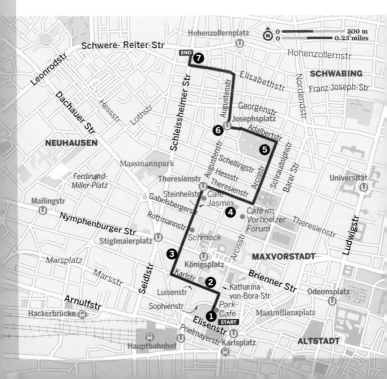

❶ Alter Botanischer Garten

The Old Botanical Garden (p73) is a pleasant, rather bushy park centred around a large sculptural fountain – a verdant oasis in a traffic-heavy part of town. There are acres of bench space here for picnickers or you could head to the Park Cafe, a less-known beer garden, but one that's frequented by locals.

❷ St Bonifaz Church

Established by King Ludwig I in 1835, this neo-Renaissance red-brick and stone church is fronted by eight classical columns. That's unusual enough in Munich, but the interior is an even bigger surprise: the pews form a circle around the altar, there is abstract art on the walls and the organ looks like it's made from bits of BMW engine.

❸ Augustenstrasse

There are two eateries to look out for on busy Augustenstrasse. The former Jewish restaurant **Schmock** at No 52 (now the Vu Tang Laos noodle house) has an ornate original interior. Up the road, on the corner with Steinheilstrasse, **Cafe Jasmin** (www.cafe-jasmin. com) takes you back to the days of the *Wirtschaftswunder* (West Germany's post-war economic recovery).

❹ Munich Technical University

Munich's 'other' university is one of Germany's best, turning out graduates that contribute to the country's engineering prowess. You should come here for the modern rooftop **Café im Vorhoelzer Forum**, which has some of the best views of any Munich eatery.

❺ Alter Nordfriedhof

You might think this overgrown **graveyard** was the last place you'd want to hang out. However, the joggers, mums with prams, and running kids give the game away. After just 71 years, the Nazis decommissioned this 19th-century cemetery, and following WWII it became a park – just one with lots of gravestones...

❻ Josephsplatz

Dominating Josephsplatz, the oversized neo-baroque St Joseph Church looks older than it is, having only been built in 1898. Inside, it's a mammoth barrel of whitewashed stucco. Outside, the city has installed an interesting children's playground, and there's a dribbling fountain you can watch from the benches.

❼ Nordbard

The Nordbad is a Munich swimming pool with an old exterior but a fully modernised interior. It's one of the least frequented pools and is open from very early morning till late at night. However, you don't have to don trunks to access the adjacent Cafe Bellevue.

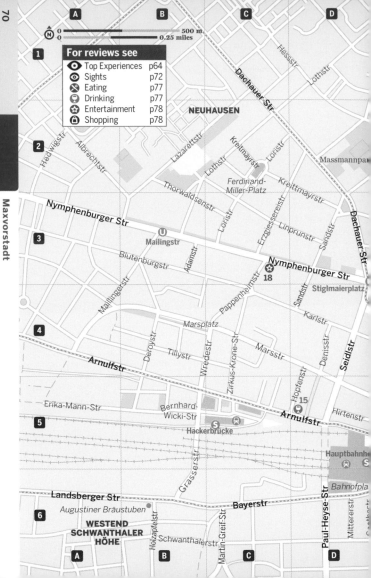

| | A | B | C | D |

For reviews see

0   500 m
0   0.25 miles

NEUHAUSEN

Dachauer Str
Hessstr
Lothstr
Massmannpa
Dachauer Str

Hedwigstr
Albrechtstr
Lazarettstr
Lothstr
Kreitmayrstr
Loristr
Kreittmayrstr

Thorwaldsenstr
Ferdinand-Miller-Platz
Erzgiessereistr
Linprunstr
Sandstr

Nymphenburger Str
Mailingstr
Blutenburgstr
Adamstr
Pappenheimstr
Nymphenburger Str
18
Sandstr
Stiglmaierplatz

Maillingerstr
Loristr
Karlstr

Marsplatz
Marsstr
Sandstr
Denisstr
Seidlstr

Arnulfstr
Deroystr
Tillystr
Wredestr
Zirkus-Krone-Str
Hopfenstr
15
Arnulfstr
Hirtenstr

Erika-Mann-Str
Bernhard-Wicki-Str
Hackerbrücke
Hauptbahnhe
Grasserstr
Bahnofpla

Landsberger Str
Bayerstr
Paul-Heyse-Str
Mittererstr

Augustiner Bräustuben
Holzapfelstr
Schwanthalerstr
Martin-Greif-Str

WESTEND
SCHWANTHALER
HÖHE

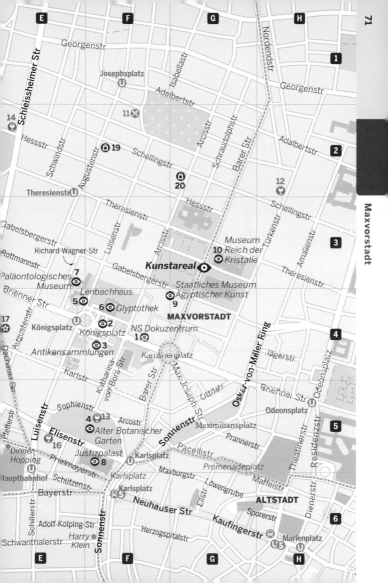

E   F   G   H

Georgenstr

Nordenstr

1

Josephsplatz
U

Isabellastr

Adalbertstr

Georgenstr

14

Schleissheimer Str

Hessstr

11 ✕

Schwindstr

Augustenstr

🔒 19   Schellingstr

Arcisstr

Schraudolphstr

Barer Str

Adalbertstr

2

🔒
20

12
⊙

Theresienstr U

Theresienstr

Hessstr

Schellingstr

Türkenstr

Amalienstr

3

Gabelsbergerstr

Luisenstr

Arcisstr

Theresienstr

Richard-Wagner-Str

Rottmannstr

Paläontologisches
Museum

Brienner Str

7

5 ⊙

Lenbachhaus

6 ⊙ Glyptothek

Gabelsbergerstr

Kunstareal ⊙

Staatliches Museum
Ägyptischer Kunst
9

Museum
10 Reich der
⊙ Kristalle

MAXVORSTADT

17
★

Königsplatz U

⊙2
Königsplatz

⊙3

Antikensammlungen

NS Dokuzentrum
1 ⊙

Oskar-von-Miller Ring

4

Karlstr

Katharina-
von-Bora-Str

Barer Str

Karolinenplatz

Max-Joseph-Str

Ottostr

Jägerstr

Odeonsplatz

Brienner Str

Dachauer Str

Augustenstr

Sophienstr

4 ⊙ 13

Arcostr

Sonnenstr

Maximiliansplatz

Odeonsplatz U

Theatinerstr

Residenzstr

5

Luisenstr

Elisenstr

16

Alter Botanischer
Garten

Justizpalast

8 ⊙

Karlsplatz U

Prannerstr

Pacellistr

Promenadeplatz

Dienerstr

Pfefferstr

Dinner
Hopping

Prielmayerstr

Maxburgstr

Maffeistr

Hauptbahnhof

Schützenstr

Karlsplatz

Löwengrube

ALTSTADT

6

Bayerstr

Karlsplatz
R S

Neuhauser Str

Elisenstr

Sporerstr

Adolf-Kolping-Str

Harry
Klein

Sonnenstr

Herzogspitalstr

Kaufingerstr

Marienplatz
U S

Schwanthalerstr

E   F   G   H

Sights

NS Dokuzentrum ARCHIVES

1 🎯 MAP P70, F4

The mission of the NS Dokuzentrum, located right at the heart of what was once Nazi central in Munich, is to educate locals and visitors alike about the Nazi period and Munich's role in it. The excellent exhibition looks to find the answers to questions such as how did Hitler come to power, what led to the war, and why did democracy fail. Period documents, artefacts, films and multimedia stations help visitors form their own understanding of this history. (National Socialism Documentation Centre; 📞089-2336 7000; www.ns-dokuzentrum-muenchen.de; Max-Mannheimer-Platz 1; adult/concession €5/2.50; 🕙10am-7pm Tue-Sun; 🚃100, Königsplatz, Ⓤ Königsplatz)

Königsplatz SQUARE

2 🎯 MAP P70, F4

Nothing less than the Acropolis in Athens provided the inspiration for Leo von Klenze's imposing Königsplatz, commissioned by Ludwig I and anchored by a Doric-columned **Propyläen** gateway and two temple-like **museums** (Antikensammlungen and Glyptothek, p75). The Nazis added a few buildings of their own and used the square for their mass parades. Only the foundations of these structures remain at the eastern end of the square, rendered unrecognisable by foliage. Peaceful and green today, the square comes

Antikensammlungen, Königsplatz

FOOTTOO/SHUTTERSTOCK ©

Football World

Sporting and architecture fans alike should take a side trip to the northern suburb of Fröttmaning to see the ultraslick €340-million **Allianz Arena** (📞 tours 089-6993 1222; www.allianz-arena.de; Werner-Heisenberg-Allee 25, Fröttmaning; tour adult/concession €19/17; 🕙 10.30am-4.30pm; Ⓤ Fröttmaning), Munich's dramatic football stadium. The 60-minute stadium tours are followed by as much time as you like in the 'Erlebnis Welt' (the Bayern Munich Experience World), the club's super-modern museum. Tickets can be booked online.

Nicknamed the life belt and the rubber boat, the stadium has walls made of inflatable cushions that can be individually lit to match the colours of the host team (red for FC Bayern, blue for TSV 1860, and white for the national side).

alive in summer during concerts and open-air cinema. (🚉 Königsplatz, Ⓤ Königsplatz)

Antikensammlungen MUSEUM

3 ⊙ MAP P70, F4

This old-school museum is an engaging showcase of exquisite Greek, Roman and Etruscan antiquities. The collection of Greek vases, each artistically decorated with gods and heroes, wars and weddings, is particularly outstanding. Other galleries present gold and silver jewellery and ornaments, figurines made from terracotta and more precious bronze, and superfragile glass drinking vessels. Tickets for the museum are also valid for the Glyptothek (p75). (www.antike-am-koenigsplatz.mwn.de; Königsplatz 1; adult/child €6/free, Sun €1; 🕙 10am-5pm Tue & Thu-Sun, to 8pm Wed; 🚉 Königsplatz, Ⓤ Königsplatz)

Alter Botanischer Garten PARK

4 ⊙ MAP P70, F5

The Old Botanical Garden is a pleasant place to soothe soles and souls after an Altstadt shopping spree or to see out a long wait for a train away from the Hauptbahnhof. Created under King Maximilian in 1814, most of the tender specimens were moved in the early 20th century to the New Botanical Garden behind Schloss Nymphenburg, leaving this island of city-centre greenery. (Sophienstrasse 7; 🕙 24hr; Ⓢ Karlsplatz, 🚉 Karlsplatz, 🚉 Karlsplatz)

Lenbachhaus MUSEUM

5 ⊙ MAP P70, E4

With its fabulous wing added by noted architect Norman Foster, this glorious gallery is the go-to place to admire the

Worth a Trip: Neuschwanstein

Appearing through the mountaintops like a mirage, **Schloss Neuschwanstein** (☏ tickets 08362-930 830; www.neuschwanstein.de; Neuschwansteinstrasse 20; adult/child €13/free, incl Hohenschwangau €25/free; ⊙ 9am-6pm Apr–mid-Oct, 10am-4pm mid-Oct–Mar) is one of the most popular day trips from Munich and it's easy to see why. King Ludwig II planned this fairy-tale pile himself, with the help of a stage designer rather than an architect. He envisioned it as a giant stage on which to recreate the world of Germanic mythology, inspired by the operatic works of his friend Richard Wagner. The castle later inspired a certain Walt Disney when building his Sleeping Beauty Castle.

Built as a romantic medieval castle, work started in 1869 and, like so many of Ludwig's grand schemes, was never finished. For all the coffer-depleting sums spent on it, the king spent just over 170 days in residence.

Completed sections include Ludwig's Tristan and Isolde–themed bedroom, dominated by a huge Gothic-style bed crowned with intricately carved cathedral-like spires; a gaudy artificial grotto (another allusion to Tannhäuser); and the Byzantine-style Thronsaal (Throne Room) with an incredible mosaic floor containing over two million stones. The painting opposite the (throneless) throne platform depicts another castle dreamed up by Ludwig that was never built (he planned many more). Almost every window provides tour-halting views across the plain below.

King Ludwig II grew up at the sun-yellow **Schloss Hohenschwangau** (☏ 08362-930 830; www.hohenschwangau.de; Alpseestrasse 30; adult/child €13/free, incl Neuschwanstein €25/free; ⊙ 8am-5pm Apr–mid-Oct, 9am-3pm mid-Oct–Mar) and later enjoyed summers here until his death in 1886. His father, Maximilian II, built this palace in a neo-Gothic style atop 12th-century ruins left by Schwangau knights. Far less showy than Neuschwanstein, Hohenschwangau has a distinctly lived-in feel where every piece of furniture is a used original. After his father died, Ludwig's main alteration was having stars, illuminated with hidden oil lamps, painted on the ceiling of his bedroom.

If you want to do the castles in a day from Munich, you'll need to start early. The first train leaves Munich at 4.48am (€28.40, change in Kaufbeuren), reaching Füssen at 6.49am. Otherwise, direct trains leave Munich once every two hours.

vibrant canvases of Kandinsky, Franz Marc, Paul Klee and other members of ground-breaking modernist group Der Blaue Reiter (The Blue Rider), founded in Munich in 1911. (Municipal Gallery; ☏089-2333 2000; www.lenbachhaus. de; Luisenstrasse 33; adult/child incl audioguide €10/5; ⊙10am-8pm Tue, to 6pm Wed-Sun; 🚊Königsplatz, Ⓤ Königsplatz)

Glyptothek
MUSEUM

6 ◉ MAP P70, F4

If you're a fan of classical art or simply enjoy the sight of naked guys without noses (or other pertinent body parts), make a beeline for the Glyptothek. One of Munich's oldest museums, it's a feast of art and sculpture from ancient

Greece and Rome amassed by Ludwig I between 1806 and 1830, and it opens a surprisingly naughty window onto the ancient world. Tickets for the museum are also valid for the Antikensammlungen (p73). (www.antike-am-koenigsplatz. mwn.de; Königsplatz 3; adult/child €6/free, Sun €1; ⊙10am-5pm Fri-Sun, Tue & Wed, to 8pm Thu; 🚊Königsplatz, Ⓤ Königsplatz)

Paläontologisches Museum
MUSEUM

7 ◉ MAP P70, E3

The curatorial concept of the Paläontologisches Museum could use a little dusting up, but otherwise this archaeological trove of prehistoric skulls and bones is anything but stuffy. The most

Schloss Neuschwanstein

VOPFASIN MONOCHIM/SHUTTERSTOCK © COURTESY OF THE BAVARIAN

Bavarian Beer Hall

Depending on the wind direction, the bitter-sweet aroma of hops envelops you as you approach the **Augustiner Bräustuben** (Map p70, B6; ☎089-507 047; www.braeustuben.de; Landsberger Strasse 19; ⏱10am-midnight; 🚊Holzapfelstrasse), a traditional beer hall inside the Augustiner brewery. The Bavarian fare is superb, especially the *Schweinshaxe* (pork knuckle). Due to the location beyond the Hauptbahnhof, the atmosphere in the evenings is slightly more authentic than that of its city-centre cousins, with fewer tourists at the long tables.

famous resident is a fossilised archaeopteryx, the creature that forms an evolutionary link between reptile and bird. (Palaeontological Museum; www.palmuc.de; Richard-Wagner-Strasse 10; admission free; ⏱8am-4pm Mon-Thu, to 2pm Fri; 🚊Königsplatz, Ⓤ Königsplatz)

Justizpalast   NOTABLE BUILDING

8 ◉ MAP P70, F5

The 1890s Justizpalast witnessed the Weisse Rose trial of Hans Scholl, Sophie Scholl and Christoph Probst on 22 February 1943. They were condemned to death by the notorious judge Roland Freisler. The verdict was read at 1pm. Four hours later they were dead. There's a permanent exhibit about the sham trial in the very courtroom (room 253) where it took place. (Palace of Justice; Prielmayerstrasse 7; admission free; ⏱9am-4pm Dec–mid-Apr & May–mid-Oct; 🚊Karlsplatz, Ⓢ Karlsplatz, Ⓤ Karlsplatz)

Staatliches Museum Ägyptischer Kunst   MUSEUM

9 ◉ MAP P70, G4

This small museum of late-19th-century Egyptian finds was moved to a purpose-built site in 2013. The 21st-century-style curation has left things feeling sparse, but there's still a lot to learn here about the 5000 years the pharaohs ruled what is now Egypt and Sudan. (Egyptian Art Museum; www.smaek.de; Gabelsbergerstrasse 35; adult/child €7/free; ⏱10am-8pm Tue, to 6pm Wed-Sun)

Museum Reich der Kristalle   MUSEUM

10 ◉ MAP P70, G3

If diamonds are your best friends, head to the Museum Reich der Kristalle, with its Fort Knox–worthy collection of gemstones and crystals, including a giant Russian emerald and meteorite fragments from Kansas. (www.mineralogische-staatssammlung.de; Theresienstrasse

41; adult/child €4/2; ⊙1-5pm
Tue-Sun; 🚇Maxvorstadt/Sammlung
Brandhorst, 🚇Pinakotheken)

Eating

Il Mulino   ITALIAN €€

🕚 11 ❌ MAP P70, F2

This much-loved neighbourhood classic has been feeding
Italophiles and immigrants from
the beautiful country for over
three decades. All the expected
pastas and pizzas are present
and correct, though the daily
specials will likely tickle the pal-
ate of more curious eaters.
Somewhat surprisingly 'The Mill'
was declared Bavarian restaurant of the year in 2017. (www.
ristorante-ilmulino.de; Görresstrasse
1; mains €6 20; ⊙11.30am-midnight;
⑤ Josephsplatz)

Drinking

Alter Simpl   PUB

12 🟢 MAP P70, H?

Thomas Mann and Hermann
Hesse used to knock 'em back
at this well-scuffed and wood-
panelled thirst parlour. A bookish
ambience still pervades, making
this an apt spot at which to curl
up with a weighty tome over a few
Irish ales. The curious name is an
abbreviation of the satirical maga-
zine *Simplicissimus*. (📞089-272
3083; www.altersimpl.com; Türkenstrasse 57; ⊙11am-3am Mon-Fri, to
4am Sat & Sun; 🚇Schellingstrasse)

Park-Cafe   BEER GARDEN

13 🟢 MAP P70, F5

A hidden gem, this typical Munich
beer garden in the Alter Botanischer Garten serves Hofbräu
suds and lots of filling food. (www.
parkcafe089.de; Sophienstrasse 7;
⊙11am-11pm; 🚇Lenbachplatz)

Eat the Rich   BAR

14 🟢 MAP P70, E2

Strong cocktails served in half-litre
glasses quickly loosen inhibitions
at this sizzling nightspot, a great
place to crash when the party's
winding down everywhere else.
Food is served till 3am on weekends. (www.eattherich.de; Hessstrasse
90; ⊙7pm-1am Thu, to 4am Fri & Sat;
Ⓤ Theresienstrasse)

> ### Dinner Hopping 🍽️
> **Dinner Hopping** (Map p70,
> E5; www.dinnerhopping.de; Ar-
> nulfstrasse 1, departure & arrival
> point next to the Hauptbahnhof;
> dinner experience from €129;
> ⊙6.30-10.15pm; 🚇Hauptbahn-
> hof, ⓊHauptbahnhof, ⑤Haupt-
> bahnhof) involves being driven
> around Munich in an old
> yellow US school bus as you
> enjoy either an Italian, Ameri-
> can or Bavarian three-course
> dinner to the accompaniment
> of a live act. It may sound
> gimmicky, but the food gets
> rave reviews.

Lights & Music 🎧

Follow the gold-lined passageway off Sonnenstrasse to **Harry Klein** (Map p70, F6; 📞089-4028 7400; www.harrykleinclub.de; Sonnenstrasse 8; ⏱from 11pm; 🚋Karlsplatz, 🅂Karlsplatz, 🅄Karlsplatz), a night spot some regard as one of the best Elektro-clubs in the world. Nights here are an amazing alchemy of electro sound and visuals, with live video art projected onto the walls Kraftwerk-style and blending to awe-inspiring effect with the music.

Augustiner Keller   BEER GARDEN

15 🚋 MAP P70, D5

Every year this leafy 5000-seat beer garden, about 500m west of the Hauptbahnhof, buzzes with fairy-lit thirst-quenching activity from the first sign that spring may have *gesprungen*. The ancient chestnuts are thick enough to seek refuge under when it rains, or else lug your mug to the actual beer cellar. Small playground. (www.augustinerkeller.de; Arnulfstrasse 52; ⏱10am-1am Apr-Oct; 👣; 🚋Hopfenstrasse)

NY Club   CLUB

16 🚋 MAP P70, E5

After a move to near the Old Botanical Gardens, it's again 'Raining Men' at Munich's hottest gay dance temple, where you can party away with Ibiza-style abandon on the cool main floor. (www.nyclub.de; Elisenstrasse 3; ⏱11pm-7am Thu-Sat; 🚋Hauptbahnhof, 🅄Hauptbahnhof, 🅂Hauptbahnhof)

Entertainment

Münchner Theater für Kinder   THEATRE

17 ⭐ MAP P70, E4

At the Münchner Theater für Kinder, budding theatre-goers can enjoy fairy tales and children's classics à la *Max & Moritz* and *Pinocchio*. (📞089-594 545; www.mtfk.de; Dachauer Strasse 46; ⏱3pm daily, 10am Sat, Sun & school holidays; 🚋Stiglmaierplatz)

Cinema   CINEMA

18 ⭐ MAP P70, C3

Cult cinema which shows all films in English, all the time. (📞089-555 255; www.cinema-muenchen.de; Nymphenburger Strasse 31; 🅄Stiglmaierplatz)

Shopping

Munich Readery   BOOKS

19 🔒 MAP P70, F2

Home to Germany's biggest collection of secondhand English-language titles, the Readery is the place to go in Bavaria for holiday reading matter. In fact, we think this might be the only such secondhand bookshop located between Paris and Prague. The shop also holds events including author readings, and there's a monthly book club. Check out the website for details. (www.readery.de; Augustenstrasse 104; ⊙11am-8pm Mon-Fri, 10am-6pm Sat; ⓊTheresienstrasse)

Holareidulijö

20 🔒 MAP P70, G2

This rare secondhand traditional-clothing store (the name is a phonetic yodel) is worth a look even if you don't intend buying. Apparently, wearing hand-me-down Lederhosen greatly reduces the risk of chafing. (www.holareidulijoe.com; Schellingstrasse 81; ⊙noon-6.30pm Tue-Fri, 10am-1pm Sat May-Sep, 2-6pm Thu & Fri, 11am-1pm Sat Oct-Apr; 🚊Schellingstrasse)

Top Experience 📷
Pay Your Respects at
KZ-Gedenkstätte Dachau

A short S-Bahn ride from central Munich, the small town of Dachau is infamous as the site of the Nazis' first concentration camp, established in 1933 and a blueprint for the many that were to follow. Half a day in Dachau is a soberingly thought-provoking experience and certainly not suitable for children. Munich tour companies make the run out here, but the trip is easy to organise on your own.

Dachau Concentration Camp Memorial Site

📞 08131-669 970

www.kz-gedenkstaette-dachau.de

Peter-Roth-Strasse 2a, Dachau

admission free

🕙 9am-5pm

Horrific First

Officially called the KZ-Gedenkstätte Dachau, this was the Nazis' first concentration camp, built by Heinrich Himmler in March 1933 to house political prisoners. All in all, it 'processed' more than 200,000 inmates, killing at least 43,000, and is now a haunting memorial. Expect to spend two to three hours here to fully absorb the exhibits.

Museum

You pass into the compound itself through the Jourhaus (entrance building) – set in wrought iron, the infamous, chilling slogan 'Arbeit Macht Frei' (Work Sets You Free) hits you at the gate.

The museum is at the southern end of the camp. Here, a 22-minute English-language documentary runs at 10am, 11.30am, 12.30pm, 2pm and 3pm and uses mostly post-liberation footage to outline what took place here. Either side of the small cinema extends an exhibition relating the camp's harrowing story. Some of the displays are extremely disturbing.

The Camp

Outside, in the former roll-call square, is the International Memorial (1968), inscribed in English, French, Yiddish, German and Russian, which reads 'Never Again'. Behind the exhibit building, the bunker was the notorious camp prison where inmates were tortured. Executions took place in the prison yard.

Inmates were housed in large barracks, now demolished, which used to line the main road north of the roll-call square. In the camp's northwestern corner is the crematorium and gas chamber, disguised as a shower room but never used. Several religious shrines stand nearby.

★ Getting There

The S2 makes the trip from the Hauptbahnhof to the station in Dachau in 22 minutes. You'll need a two-zone ticket (€5.80). Here change to bus 726 alighting at the KZ-Gedenkstätte stop.

★ Top Tips

o A trip to Dachau isn't recommended for children under 12 years old.

o Dachau is one of the few sights in or around Munich that's easy to visit by car.

o The bookshop in the visitors centre has many books in English for those who want to learn more.

✖ Take a Break

The cafe at the visitors centre is open from 9am to 5pm and serves snacks, coffees and cakes.

Explore ✦

Schwabing & the Englischer Garten

Once the haunt of Kandinsky and Mann, fashionable Schwabing remains a pleasant place to stroll. The area has some of the highest rents in town and is populated by well-heeled professionals who live in beautifully restored Jugendstil (art nouveau) buildings. This is also a student area – the neighbourhood's south bustles with uni life and undergraduates laze on the lawns of the huge Englischer Garten.

Schwabing is split into three sections: the residential north; the studenty south; and the Englischer Garten. Spend your morning in the latter, strolling the widescreen lawns, scrambling through the follies and perhaps taking a rowboat out onto the Kleinhesseloher See. Grab lunch at the tree-shaded Hirschau beer garden before heading to the Bayerisches Nationalmuseum and/or the fascinating Haus der Kunst, Hitler's purpose-built gallery. End the day in the student area where aimless wandering will take you to many a cafe, bar, bookshop and vintage-clothing store.

Getting There & Around

Ⓤ The U3 and U6 stop at Universität, Giselastrasse and Münchner Freiheit, all on Ludwigstrasse/Leopoldstrasse.

🚌 Service 100 stops along the southern end of the Englischer Garten.

Neighbourhood Map on p88

Siegestor (p91) FHM/GETTY IMAGES ©

Top Experience 📷
Picnic in the Englischer Garten

The sprawling English Garden is among Europe's biggest city parks – it even rivals London's Hyde Park and New York's Central Park for size – and is a popular playground for locals and visitors alike. Stretching north from Prinzregentenstrasse for about 5km, it was commissioned by Elector Karl Theodor in 1789. It's a superb place to escape Munich's hullabaloo to ride a bike, picnic or just laze on the grass.

◉ **MAP P88, C5**

English Garden

Ⓤ Universität

South Park

The very south of the Englischer Garten is argu-ably its most interesting part. Here you can join the groups of spectators leaning over a bridge to watch surfers riding the Eisbach's artificial wave (p89). Or wriggle into a wetsuit and have a go yourself. All this goes on in the shadow of the Haus der Kunst (p90), the gallery Hitler fa-mously built to display Nazi-approved art. Just behind the gallery is the **Japanisches Teehaus**, built for the 1972 Olympics, by an idyllic duck pond.

Park Follies

Two towering pieces of folly architecture domi-nate the park's middle section. Rising above the main lawns is the Monopteros (p90; 1838), a small Greek temple with interesting views of the city centre. A short walk north brings you to the Chinesischer Turm (p95), another folly, though this time in the shape of a multi-tiered Chinese pagoda. This is the unlikely setting for Munich's oldest beer garden.

Northern Stretches

The further north you go, the wilder the English Garden becomes, though there are two spots where nature has been tamed for human enjoy-ment. The Kleinhesseloher See (p90) is a lovely lake where you can boat around three little islands, then rewarding your efforts with a beer at the Seehaus (p97). Some day soon a tunnel will take the motorway just north of the lake under the greenery, reuniting the two halves of the park. For now a footbridge is needed to reach the Hirschau (p97) beer garden, one of Munich's best.

★ Top Tips

● If you are short on time, some Munich tour agencies run cycling tours of the English Garden.

● Many commut-ers cycle through the garden at high speeds – take care of children on the main paths.

● A section of the Berlin Wall lurks hidden between the Haus der Kunst and the US Consulate.

✕ Take a Break

The Chinesischer Turm (p95) beer garden is the place to call a halt in the park.

Hirschau (p97) is a huge beer garden in the northern half of the English Garden.

Walking Tour

Bohemian Bolthole

Centred around the University and the Art Academy, this erstwhile bolthole for 19th- and early-20th-century artists and writers still has a bohemian feel, despite much postwar gentrification. Join the students for a bite to eat, peruse vintage-clothes shops and admire the art nouveau architecture in Schwabing, Munich's most characterful quarter.

Walking Facts

Start Munich University; Ⓤ Universität

End Wedekind-Platz; Ⓤ Münchner Freiheit

❶ Munich University

From morning till dusk the area around Munich's Ludwig Maxmilian University bustles with students, many of whom tie up their rattling two-wheelers along Ludwig Strasse. The top attraction for visitors within the uni building is the DenkStätte Weisse Rose (p90), a couple of rooms dedicated to students who were executed for distributing anti-Nazi leaflets.

❷ Schellingstrasse

Running next to the uni, Schellingstrasse funnels students to various watering and feeding spots throughout the day. In addition to its many cafes, it's also the location of Words' Worth Books (p97), the city's best English bookstore, and the uni bookshop.

❸ Amalienstrasse

Running north–south, Amalienstrasse bustles like a United Nations of edibles, with cafes, delis and restaurants that serve a multitude of cuisines lining its arrow-straight length. It's one of the best places to head come the lunching hour, though things get very busy with hungry students.

❹ Türkenstrasse

Türkenstrasse is the place to head for more interesting shops, including shops stocking antiques and vintage clothes, and even an Oxfam shop at No 81. But the highlight here is Alter Simpl (p77), one of Munich's most famous historical pubs where Thomas Mann, Hermann Hesse and many other Schwabing writers, poets and artists once drank.

❺ Leopoldpark

Take a break at this neighbourhood park, especially good for kiddies with its large playground. Normally packed with students from the nearby Art Academy lazing on the grass or writing a last-minute essay, it's a relaxing place to occupy a bench and soak up the atmosphere.

❻ Ainmillerstrasse

Schwabing becomes more gentrified the further north you stroll, but it wasn't that way when Wassily Kandinsky and Rainer Maria Rilke lived at Nos 36 and 34 respectively on Ainmillerstrasse. Seek out their brass plaques, admire the perfectly renovated art nouveau facades, then head east.

❼ Wedekind-Platz & Around

Beyond the Münchner Freiheit transport hub, the area around Wedekind-Platz is a real nightlife hotspot, with bars, cafes and quirky German-language comedy theatres aplenty. On Wedekind-Platz, look out for the crooked lamp post, the **Schwabinger Laterne**, once made famous by local chanson singer, Schwabinger Gisela.

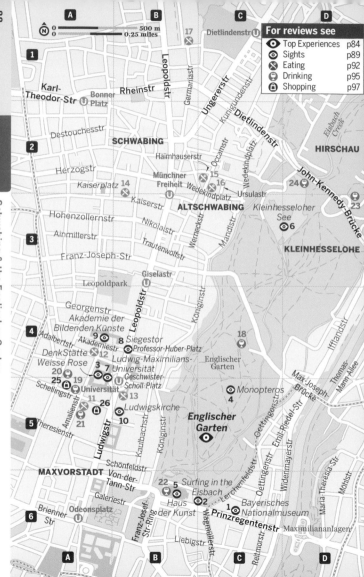

For reviews see
- Top Experiences p84
- Sights p89
- Eating p92
- Drinking p95
- Shopping p97

17
Dietlindenstr

Karl-Theodor-Str
Bonner Platz
Rheinstr
Leopoldstr
Germaniastr
Ungererstr
Kunigundenstr
Dietlindenstr
Eisbach Creek
HIRSCHAU
John-Kennedy-Brücke

Destouchesstr
SCHWABING
Haimhauserstr
Occamstr
Wedekindplatz
24

Herzogstr
Münchner Freiheit
14 Kaiserplatz
15
16
Wedekindplatz
Ursulastr
Kleinhesseloher See
6
23

Kaiserstr
ALTSCHWABING
KLEINHESSELOHE

Hohenzollernstr
Nikolaistr
Werneckstr
Mandlstr

Ainmillerstr
Trautenwolfstr

Franz-Joseph-Str
Giselastr
Leopoldstr

Leopoldpark

Georgenstr
Akademie der Bildenden Künste
9
8 Siegestor
18
Adalbertstr
Akademiestr
Professor-Huber-Platz
Englischer Garten

DenkStätte
12
Ludwig-Maximilians-
Weisse Rose
20
3 7 Universität
Geschwister-
25
19 Universität
Scholl-Platz
13
Schellingstr
11 26

Amalienstr
10 Ludwigskirche
21

Theresienstr
Ludwigstr
Königinstr
Kaulbachstr

Monopteros
4

Englischer Garten

Max-Joseph-Brücke
Oettingenstr
Emil-Riedel-Str
Ifflandstr
Thomas-Mann-Allee
Max-Joseph-
Brücke

MAXVORSTADT
Schönfeldstr
Von-der-Tann-Str
Galeriestr

Brienner Str
Odeonsplatz
22 5 Surfing in the Eisbach
Haus der Kunst
1
2 Prinzregentenstr
Bayerisches Nationalmuseum
Maximilliananlagen

Franz-Josef-Str-Ring
Liebigstr
Lerchenfeldstr
Wagmüllerstr
Reitmorstr
Widenmayerstr
Maria-Theresia-Str
Möhlstr

Sights

Bayerisches Nationalmuseum   MUSEUM

1 ◎ MAP P88, C6

Picture the classic 19th-century museum, a palatial neoclassical edifice overflowing with exotic treasure and thought-provoking works of art, a repository for a nation's history, a grand purpose-built display case for royal trinkets, church baubles and state-owned rarities – this is the Bavarian National Museum, a good old-fashioned institution for no-nonsense museum lovers. As the collection fills 40 rooms over three floors, there's a lot to get through here, so be prepared for at least two hours' legwork. (www.

bayerisches-nationalmuseum.de; Prinzregentenstrasse 3; adult/concession/child €7/6/free, Sun €1; ◷10am-5pm Tue, Wed & Fri-Sun, to 8pm Thu; ⬚Nationalmuseum/Haus Der Kunst, ⬚Nationalmuseum/Haus Der Kunst)

Surfing in the Eisbach   SURFING

2 ◎ MAP P88, C6

At the southern tip of the Englischer Garten, you'll see scores of people leaning over a bridge to cheer on wetsuit-clad daredevils as they 'hang 10' on an artificially created wave in the Eisbach. It's only a single wave, but it's a damn fine one. The surfers are such an attraction that the tourist office includes them in its brochures. (www.eisbachwelle.de; Prinzregentenstrasse; ⬚Nationalmuseum/Haus der Kunst)

DenkStätte Weisse Rose (p90)

DenkStätte Weisse Rose

MEMORIAL

3 🔘 MAP P88, A4

This memorial exhibit to the *Weisse Rose* (White Rose; a non-violent resistance group led by Munich University students Hans and Sophie Scholl to oppose the Nazis) is within the Ludwig-Maximilians-Universität. It's a moving story, and one of Munich's most heroic, told in photographs and exhibits from the period. (www.weisse-rose-stiftung.de; Geschwister-Scholl-Platz 1; admission free; ⏰10am-5pm Mon-Fri, 11am-4.30pm Sat; U Universität)

Monopteros

NOTABLE BUILDING

4 🔘 MAP P88, C5

At the top of a gentle hill in the Englischer Garten stands the heavily photographed Monopteros (1838), a small Greek temple built by 19th-century star architect, Leo von Klenze. From here you can admire the view of the Munich sky-line, which is particularly attractive at sunset. (Englischer Garten)

Haus der Kunst

MUSEUM

5 🔘 MAP P88, B6

This austere fascist-era edifice was built in 1937 to showcase Nazi art, but now the Haus der Kunst presents works by exactly the art-ists whom the Nazis rejected and deemed degenerate. Temporary shows focus on contemporary art and design. (House of Art; www.haus derkunst.de; Prinzregentenstrasse 1; adult/concession €12/5; ⏰10am-8pm Fri-Wed, to 10pm Thu; 🚇National-museum/Haus Der Kunst, 🚊National-museum/Haus Der Kunst)

Kleinhesseloher See

LAKE

6 🔘 MAP P88, D3

Sooner or later in the Englischer Garten you'll find your way to the Kleinhesseloher See, a lovely lake at the centre of the park. Work up a sweat while taking a spin around three little islands, then quaff a well-earned foamy one at the See-haus beer garden (p97). (Englischer Garten; U Universität)

Ludwig-Maximilians-Universität

UNIVERSITY

7 🔘 MAP P88, A4

Bavaria's oldest university, the Ludwig-Maximilians-Universität started out as a political football for its rulers. Founded in Ingolstadt in 1472, the university moved to Landshut in 1800 before being shifted to Munich in 1826 by newly crowned King Ludwig I. It has produced more than a dozen Nobel Prize winners, including Wilhelm Röntgen in 1901 (Physics) and Theodor Hänsch in 2005 (Physics).The **main building**, by Friedrich von Gärtner of course, has cathedral-like dimensions and is accented with sculpture and other artworks. A flight of stairs leads to a light court with a memo-rial to *Die Weisse Rose,* the Nazi resistance group founded by Hans and Sophie Scholl. To get the full story, visit the small DenkStätte in the vaulted space behind. (LMU;

The White Rose Resistance Movement

Open resistance to the Nazis was rare during the Third Reich; after 1933, intimidation and the instant 'justice' of the Gestapo and SS served as powerful disincentives. One of the few groups to rebel was the ill-fated *Weisse Rose* (White Rose), led by Munich University student siblings Hans and Sophie Scholl.

The nonviolent White Rose began operating in 1942, its members stealing out at night to smear 'Freedom!' and 'Down with Hitler!' on the city's walls. Soon they were printing anti-Nazi leaflets on the mass extermination of the Jews and other Nazi atrocities. One read: 'We shall not be silent – we are your guilty conscience. The White Rose will not leave you in peace'.

In February 1943, Hans and Sophie were caught distributing leaflets at the university. Together with their best friend, Christoph Probst, the Scholls were arrested and charged with treason. After a summary trial, all three were found guilty and beheaded the same afternoon. Their extraordinary courage inspired the award-winning film *Sophie Scholl – Die Letzten Tage* (Sophie Scholl – The Final Days; 2005).

A memorial exhibit to the White Rose, DenkStätte is within the Ludwig-Maximilian-Universität.

Schwabing & the Englischer Garten Sights

www.uni-muenchen.de; Geschwister-Scholl-Platz 1, **S** Universität)

Siegestor
HISTORIC BUILDING

8 ◉ MAP P88, B4

Munich's massive Siegestor was modelled on the Arch of Constantine in Rome and looks like a miniature version of the Arc de Triomphe in Paris. Built to honour the Bavarian army for sending Napoleon packing, it's crowned by a triumphant Bavaria piloting a lion-drawn chariot. Severely damaged in WWII, the arch was turned into a peace memorial. The inscription on the upper section reads: *Dem Sieg geweiht, vom Kriege zerstört,* *zum Frieden mahnend* (Dedicated to victory, destroyed by war, calling for peace). (Victory Gate; Ludwig-strasse; **S** Universität)

Akademie der Bildenden Künste
ARTS CENTRE

9 ◉ MAP P88, A4

The Academy of Fine Arts is housed in a three-storey neo-Renaissance building. Founded in 1808 by Maximilian I, it advanced to become one of Europe's leading arts schools in the second half of the 19th century and still has a fine reputation today. (Academy of Fine Arts; ☎ 089-385 20; www.adbk.de; Akademiestrasse 2-4; **S** Universität)

Ludwigskirche
CHURCH

10 MAP P88, B5

The sombre twin-towered Lud-wigskirche, built by Friedrich von Gärtner between 1829 and 1844, is a highly decorative, almost Byzantine, affair with one major showpiece: the *Last Judgment* fresco by the Nazarene painter Peter Cornelius in the choir. It's one of the largest in the world and an immodest – and thoroughly unsuccessful – attempt to outdo Michelangelo's version. (Church of St Ludwig; Ludwigstrasse 20; ⏰8am-8pm; **S**Universität)

Eating

Pommes Boutique
FAST FOOD €

11 MAP P88, A5

This funky decade-old lunch halt serves cheap-as-chips Belgian-style fries made from organic potatoes, 30-odd finger-licking dips to dunk them in, pulled pork, and *Currywurst* to die for. (Amalienstrasse 46; mains €3.70-11; ⏰10am-10pm Mon-Sat, noon-8pm Sun; **U**Universität)

Bar Tapas
TAPAS €

12 MAP P88, A4

A phalanx of 30 tapas – *boquer-ones* (anchovies) to octopus salad to garlic chicken – reports for duty behind glass along the bar of this convivial Iberian outpost. Write down the numbers, then sit back with a jug of sangria and wait for your tasty morsels to arrive. (☎089-390 919; www.bar-tapas.com; Amalienstrasse 97; tapas each around €5; ⏰5pm-1am; 🍴; **S**Universität)

Cafe an der Uni
CAFE €

13 MAP P88, B5

Anytime is a good time to be at charismatic CADU. Enjoy breakfast (served until a hangover-friendly 10pm!), a cuppa Java or a Helles in the lovely garden hidden by a wall from busy Ludwigstrasse. (Ludwigstrasse 24; mains around €9; ⏰8am-1am Mon-Fri, from 9am Sat & Sun; 📶🍴; **S**Universität)

Cochinchina
ASIAN €€

14 MAP P88, B2

Bearing an old name for southern Vietnam, this cosmopolitan Asian

Tantris (p94)

TRAVELCOLLECTION/ALAMY STOCK PHOTO ©

Degenerate Art

Expressionism, surrealism, Dadaism...modern art of all stripes was anathema to Hitler and his honchos. Internationally renowned artists such as Klee, Beckmann and Schlemmer were forced into exile, their work was removed from museums and confiscated from private collections. The Nazis then sold off the works to rake in foreign currency; about 4000 works were publicly burned in Berlin.

However, in July 1937 Goebbels gathered about 650 paintings, sculptures and prints in the cramped and poorly lit Galerie am Hofgarten, calling it an exhibit of *Entartete Kunst* (Degenerate Art). Organised into such themes as Mockery of God and Insult to German Womanhood, it was intended to portray modern art as debauched and decadent. The propaganda show opened on 19 July 1937, just one day after the Great German Art Exhibition of Nazi-approved works premiered in the nearby, custom-built Haus der Deutschen Kunst. Ironically, the Nazi art was largely reviled by the public, while over two million people came to see the *Entartete Kunst,* more than any other modern art show in history.

fusion restaurant is Munich's top place for Vietnamese and Chinese concoctions. The food is consumed in a dark, dramatically exotic space devoted to the firefly and splashed with colour in the shape of Chinese vases and lamps. The traditional *pho* soup is southern Germany's best. (☏089-3898 9577; www.cochinchina.de; Kaiserstrasse 28; mains around €20; ⊙11.30am-2.30pm & 6pm-midnight; ☏; Ⓤ Münchner Freiheit)

Potting Shed

BURGERS €€

15 ⊗ MAP P88, C2

This relaxed hang-out serves tapas, gourmet burgers and cocktails to an easygoing evening crowd. The burger menu whisks you round the globe, but it's the 'Potting Shed Special', involving an organic beef burger flambéed in whisky, that catches the eye on the simple but well-concocted menu. (www.thepottingshed.de; Occamstrasse 11; mains €5-18; ⊙from 6pm Tue-Sat; Ⓤ Münchner Freiheit)

Ruff's Burger & BBQ

BURGERS €€

16 ⊗ MAP P88, C2

Munich's obsession with putting a bit of fried meat between two buns is celebrated at this Schwabing joint, where the burgers are 100% Bavarian beef – except,

Beer Glossary

Alkoholfreies Bier – nonalcoholic beer

Bockbier/Doppelbock – strong beer (*doppel* meaning even more so), either pale, amber or dark in colour with a bittersweet flavour

Dampfbier (steam beer) – originating from Bayreuth, it's top-fermented (this means the yeast rises to the top during the fermentation process) and has a fruity flavour

Dunkles (dark lager) – a reddish-brown, full-bodied lager, malty and lightly hopped

Helles (pale lager) – a lightly hopped lager with strong malt aromas and a slightly sweet taste

Hofbräu – type of brewery belonging to a royal court

Klosterbräu – type of brewery belonging to a monastery

Malzbier – sweet, aromatic, full-bodied malt beer

Märzen – full bodied with strong malt aromas and traditionally brewed in March

Pils (pilsener) – a bottom-fermented lager with strong hop flavour

Rauchbier (smoke beer) – dark beer with a fresh, spicy or 'smoky' flavour, found mostly in Bamberg

Weissbier/Weizen (wheat beer) – wheat beers (around 5.4% alcohol) with fruity and spicy flavour, often recalling bananas and cloves; a cloudy *Hefeweizen* has a layer of still-fermenting yeast on the bottom of the bottle, whereas *Kristallweizen* is clearer with more fizz.

If you want to go easy on the booze, order a sweetish *Radler*, which comes in half or full litres and mixes *Helles Lagerbier* and lemonade. A *Russe* (Russian) is generally a litre-sized concoction of *Helles Weissbier* and lemonade.

of course, for the token veggie version. Erdinger and Tegernseer beer and mostly outdoor seating. (Occamstrasse 4; burgers €5.50-16, other mains €9-19; ⏱11.30am-11pm Mon-Wed, to midnight Thu-Sat, to 10pm Sun; 🐕; Ⓤ Münchner Freiheit)

Tantris

INTERNATIONAL €€€

17 🍴 MAP P88, B1

Tantris means 'the search for perfection' and here, at one of Germany's most famous restaurants, it's not far off it. The interior design is full-bodied '70s – all postbox reds, truffle blacks and illuminated yellows. The food is sublime and the service is sometimes as unobtrusive as it is efficient. The wine cellar is probably Germany's best. Reservations essential. (☎089-361 9590; www.tantris.de; Johann-Fichte-Strasse 7; menu from €100; ☉noon-3pm & 6.30pm-1am Tue-Sat Oct-Dec, closed Tue Jan-Sep; 🛜; Ⓤ Dietlindenstrasse)

Drinking

Chinesischer Turm   BEER GARDEN

18 🟢 MAP P88, C4

This one's hard to ignore because of its English Garden location and pedigree as Munich's oldest beer garden (open since 1791). Camera-toting tourists and laid-back locals, picnicking families and businessmen sneaking a sly brew clomp around the wooden pagoda, showered by the strained sounds of an oompah band. (☎089-383 8730; www.chinaturm.de; Englischer Garten 3; ☉10am-11pm late Apr-Oct; 🚇Chinesischer Turm, 🚊Tivolistrasse)

Schall & Rauch   BAR

19 🟢 MAP P88, A5

The few battered cafe chairs and vintage barstools get bagged quickly at this small, friendly, open-fronted bar, meaning drinkers often spill out onto Schellingstrasse even during the day. With a long menu of drinks and an easygoing feel, this is a relaxing place for lunch or a last weekend drink at 2am. (Schellingstrasse 22;

Chinesischer Turm

W.BOSTOCK CREATIVE/SHUTTERSTOCK ©

⏰10am-1am Sun-Thu, to 3am Fri & Sat; 📶; ⓊUniversität)

Cafe Zeitgeist

CAFE

20 🚇 MAP P88, A4

Go with the zeitgeist and take a pew at this perfect spot where you can enjoy a hearty breakfast or pore over coffee and cake as you watch, from a shady court-yard, the steady flow of students and hipsters wandering along Türkenstrasse. (Türkenstrasse 74; ⏰9am-1am Sun-Thu, to 3am Fri & Sat; 🚊Schellingstrasse)

Black Bean

CAFE

21 🚇 MAP P88, A5

If you thought the only decent brew Bavarians could mash was beer, train your Arabica radar to this regional retort to Starbucks. The organic coffee gets tops marks, as do the muffins. (Amalien-strasse 44; ⏰7am-7pm Mon-Fri, from 8am Sat & Sun; 📶; ⓊUniversität)

P1

CLUB

22 🚇 MAP P88, B6

If you make it past the notorious face control at Munich's premier late spot, you'll encounter a crowd of Bundesliga reserve players, Q-list celebs and quite a few Russian speakers too busy seeing and being seen to actually have a good time. But it's all part of the fun, and the decor and summer terrace have their appeal. (www.p1-club.de; Prinzregentenstrasse 1; ⏰11pm-4am Tue-Sat; 🚊Nationalmuseum/Haus der Kunst)

Seehaus

Munich's Top Architects

Asam Brothers Cosmas and Egid were two of nine children. Sent to Rome for their artistic education, they returned as masters of baroque stucco, fresco and sculpture.

François de Cuvilliés Started out as a court dwarf before being taken under the wing of Maximilian II and trained in Paris before returning as court architect.

Leo von Klenze Court architect to Ludwig I, responsible for the Greek revivalist style sported by many of Munich's grandest buildings, particularly around Königsplatz.

Friedrich von Gärtner Another of Ludwig I's favourite architects, Koblenz-born von Gärtner studied in Paris and Italy and served as artistic director of the Nymphenburg Porcelain Manufactory and the Munich Academy of Fine Arts.

Hirschau
BEER GARDEN

23 MAP P88, D3

This mammoth beer garden in the northern half of the English Garden can seat 1700 quaffers and hosts live music almost every day in the summer months. When the picnic is over, dispatch the kids to the large playground while you indulge in some tankard caressing. (www.hirschau-muenchen.de; Gysslingstrasse 15; noon-11pm Mon-Fri, from 11am Sat & Sun; Dietlindenstrasse)

Seehaus
BEER GARDEN

24 MAP P88, D2

Situated on the shores of the English Garden's Kleinhesseloher See, the Seehaus has a family-friendly beer garden with an attached almost-upmarket restaurant. (Kleinhesselohe 3; 10am-1am; Münchner Freiheit)

Shopping

Pick & Weight
CLOTHING

25 MAP P88, A5

Part of a small national chain, Pick & Weight sells top-notch vintage clothing for between €25 and €95 per kilo. The men's and women's attire, plus accessories, are of the highest quality, and the shop is crammed with exquisite yesteryear pieces. (Schellingstrasse 24; noon-8pm Mon-Sat; Universität)

Words' Worth Books
BOOKS

26 MAP P88, A5

You'll find tonnes of English-language books, from secondhand novels to the latest bestsellers, at this excellent and long-established bookstore. (www.wordsworth.de; Schellingstrasse 3; 9am-8pm Mon-Fri, 10am-4pm Sat; Schellingstrasse)

Walking Tour 🥾

Historic Munich

This engaging amble takes you from the milling crowds of the central Marienplatz to the tranquil lawns and follies of the English Garden via some of the city's most significant sights, including its two most important churches. This loop through the very heart of the Bavarian capital can be done at a gallop or you could spread out the sights over two days.

Walk Facts

Start: Marienplatz;
Ⓤ Marienplatz

End: Englisher Garten;
Ⓤ Münchner Freiheit

Length: 6km, two hours

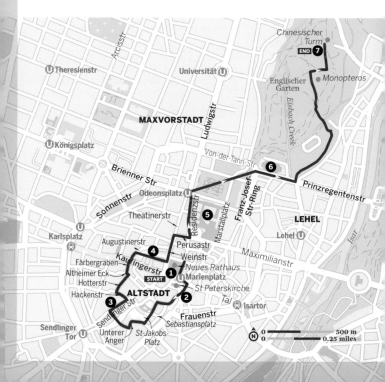

❶ Marienplatz

Epicentral Marienplatz is where many a walking tour kicks off and that's where you will start. Take the lift up the tower of the Neues Rathaus (p43), Grab a map at the tourist office, pop into the St Peterskirche (p43) and let yourself be swept along by the madding crowds who converge here to get their bearings.

❷ Viktualienmarkt

Just south of the Marienplatz another large piazza opens up, though this one is cluttered year-round with stalls (p47) selling all kinds of foodstuffs both local and imported. If you're not in the market for olives or Alpine cheese, head to the beer garden, the only one in town serving beer from all of the city's breweries.

❸ Asamkirche

Prepared to be wowed by Munich's most outrageous baroque interior (p50), created by the Asam brothers as their private chapel. A riot of cherubs, barley twist columns, faux marble and gilt sun bursts reveals itself as the eye becomes accustomed to the dingey light.

❹ Frauenkirche

Next stop is another church, the skyline dominating Frauenkirche (p50) with its two high-rise onion domes. They lord it over Munich's cityscape, as no building may be built taller. Renovation work has been taking place for years on the north tower which means you can't admire the views from the top just yet.

❺ Residenz

Home to the Bavarian royal Wittelsbach family for longer than even they could remember, the Residenz (p40) may not have had any permanaént residents since WWI, but it sure does attract a lot of temporary visitors who shuffle through its elaborate rooms in awe. It takes half a day to see everything so you may want to leave this until later.

❻ Haus der Kunst

As a failed artist Hitler was probably a big fan of galleries, and he had this one purpose-built as a propaganda showcase of works chosen by the Nazis. It's now a gallery focusing on contemporary art of the sort that the Nazis would have labelled 'degenerate' (p90).

❼ Englischer Garten

After all that urban trekking you deserve a breather, and the best place for that is among the trees, meadows and follies of the English Garden (p84), one of Europe's finest city parks. The focus of the park is the Chinesischer Turm, around which is gathered one of the world's best beer gardens, the ideal place to end your day.

Top Experience 📷
Spend a Day at the Palaces of Schleissheim

When you've exhausted all possibilities in central Munich, the northern suburb of Schleissheim is well worth the short S-Bahn trip for its three elegant palaces and a high-flying aviation museum (a branch of the Deutsches Museum, and a great way to pass a rainy afternoon). All Schleissheim sights are gathered in one location – expect to spend at least half a day to do the place justice.

www.schloesser-schleissheim.de

Maximilianshof 1

adult/concession €3/2, all 3 palaces €8/6

🕐 9am-6pm Tues-Sun Apr-Sep, 10am-4pm Oct-Mar

🚊 Mittenheimerstrasse

Neues Schloss

The highlight of Schleissheim's palatial trio is the Neues Schloss, a pompous pile dreamed up by Prince-Elector Max Emanuel in 1701 in anticipation of his promotion to emperor. However, the promotion never came. Instead he was forced into exile for over a decade and didn't get back to building until 1715. Cash-flow problems required the scaling back of the original plans but the result was still an opulent chateau.

Some of the finest artists of the baroque era were called in to create such eye-pleasing sights as the ceremonial staircase, the Victory Hall and the Grand Gallery. The particularly impressive ceiling fresco is by Cosmas Damian Asam.

The palace is home to the Staatsgalerie (State Gallery), a selection of European baroque art drawn from the Bavarian State Collection.

Schloss Lustheim & Altes Schloss

While the Neues Schloss was under construction, the elector and his retinue resided in the fanciful hunting palace of Schloss Lustheim, on a little island in the eastern Schlosspark. It now provides an elegant setting for a collection of Meissen porcelain.

The Altes Schloss is a mere shadow of its Renaissance self, having been altered and refashioned in the intervening centuries.

Flugwerft Schleissheim

The **Flugwerft Schleissheim** (www.deutsches-museum.de/flugwerft; Ferdinand-Schulz-Allee; adult/child €7/3; ⏱9am-5pm; 🚌Mittenheimerstrasse) makes for a nice change of pace and aesthetics from Schleissheim's regal palaces. Spirits will soar at the sight of the lethal Soviet MiG-21 fighter jet, the Vietnam-era F-4E Phantom and a replica of Otto Lilienthal's 1894 glider. Kids can climb into an original cockpit, land a plane and even get their pilot's licence.

★ Getting There

Take the S1 (direction Freising) to Oberschleissheim (€5.80), then walk along Mittenheimer Strasse for about 15 minutes towards the palaces. On weekdays only, bus 292 goes to the Mittenheimer Strasse stop.

★ Top Tips

o Save a bit of money by buying a ticket valid for all three palaces.

o The Flugwerft Schleisshaim is a great place to take the kids.

✕ Take a Break

The **Schloss-wirtschaft Oberschleissheim** next to the Altes Schloss is the best place to grab lunch or relax post-tour with a Helles.

Explore ◈

Haidhausen & Lehel

Haidhausen is hip, eclectic and leagues away from its 19th-century working-class roots. Major gentrification since the late 1970s has made the district desirable for artsy professionals and urban types. It's light on sights but a lovely place for aimless wandering. Lehel (lay-hl) has the second-highest concentration of museums after the art nexus in Maxvorstadt. It's the oldest Munich suburb, having been absorbed into the city in 1724, and its charismatic warren of quiet streets is lined with late-19th-century buildings.

The place to start a day in Haidhausen and Lehel is the Deutsches Museum (p104), by far the area's main attraction. Half a day is just about enough to see most of the technical wonders on display here before grabbing lunch and heading to Villa Stuck (p109), one of Europe's finest art nouveau homes, and Sammlung Schack (p109) for a dose of Romantic art. In the evening take a wander through the atmospheric streets of Lehel before ending the day at Wirtshaus in der Au (p113) for a meat and dumpling combo washed down with a Munich beer or two.

Getting There & Around

S For Lehel the U-Bahn station of the same name is the place to alight. Prinzregentenplatz and Max-Weber-Platz serve Haidhausen.

🚊 The Deutsches Museum has its own tram stop. Trams 16 and 19 serve Lehel while trams 13, 15, 18 and 37 run through Haidhausen.

Neighbourhood Map on p108

Friedensengel (p113) FOOTTOO/GETTY IMAGES ©

Top Experience 📷
Put the Kids in a Mouse Wheel at Deutsches Museum

If science is an unfathomable turn-off for you, a visit to the Deutsches Museum might just show you that physics and engineering are more fun than you thought. Spending a few hours in this temple to technology is a journey of discovery, and the exhibitions and demonstrations will be a hit with kids. You could spend a whole day wandering the museum's halls – many do.

◉ MAP P108, A4

☎ 089-217 9333

www.deutsches-museum.de

Museumsinsel 1

adult/child €12/4

🕒 9am-5pm

🚊 Deutsches Museum

Museum on an Island

Occupying the Museumsinsel (Museum Island) in the River Isar, this unrivalled museum could keep you occupied all day, especially with inquisitive kids in tow – the collections boast 100,000 items, either displayed or in storage. There are tons of interactive displays (including glass blowing and paper making), live demonstrations and experiments, model coal and salt mines, and engaging sections on cave paintings, geodesy, microelectronics and astronomy. In fact, it can be pretty overwhelming after a while, so it's best to prioritise what you want to see.

Kinderreich

The place to entertain children aged three to eight is the fabulous Kinderreich, where 1000 activities await, from a kid-size mouse wheel to interactive water fun. Get the littlies to climb all over a fire engine, build things with giant Lego, construct a waterway with canals and locks, or bang on a drum all day in a (thankfully) sound-proof instrument room.

Verkehrszentrum

The museum's second branch, the **Verkehrs-zentrum** (Transport Museum; www.deutsches-museum.de/verkehrszentrum; Am Bavariapark 5; adult/child €7/3; ⊙9am-5pm; ⓊTheresienwiese), in the west of the city centre, is an ode to the Bavarian obsession with getting around. The collections explore the ingenious ways humans have devised to transport things, including each other. From the earliest automobiles to famous race cars and the high-speed ICE trains, a visit is a virtual trip through transport history.

The exhibit is spread over three historic trade-fair halls near Theresienwiese – each with its own theme: Public Transportation, Travel, and Mobility & Technology – and is a fun place even if you can't tell a piston from a carburettor.

★ Top Tips

○ If you want to visit all three branches of the Deutsches Museum, a combi ticket costs €19.

○ Go online to view all the Deutsches Museum's collections and archives at https://digital.deutsches-museum.de/ueber.

○ This is a favourite with visiting families: leave the Kinderreich until last, as it's hard to get the little ones out of there!

○ Save time by purchasing tickets online through the museum website.

○ Tours of the main building last two hours, leave at 11am and 2pm daily, and cost €3.

✗ Take a Break

Nearby Wirtshaus in der Au (p113) is one of Munich's finest taverns.

Biergarten Muffat-werk (p115) serves meals all day.

Walking Tour 🥾

A Stroll Through Haidhausen

The suburb of Haidhausen actually predates the Altstadt by a few hundred years and was for centuries a poor area where labourers and fresh arrivals from Bavaria's hinterland would set up shop. Today it is a tranquil area of residential streets, neighbourhood businesses and dog-walking locals, but some reminders of the grittier past remain.

Walk Facts

Start Mariahilfplatz; 🚋18

End Wiener Platz; U Maz-Weber-Platz

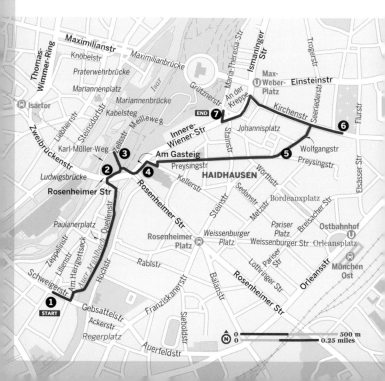

❶ Mariahilfplatz

Tram 18 drops you off at Mariahilfplatz, the venue for some of Munich's dult festivals (traditional fairs with rides and food). Passing by the red-brick Mariahilfkirche you'll come to the Auer Mühlbach, a fast-moving stream that once powered mills. You can follow it to the next stop through leafy residential areas, one on an island.

❷ Müller'sches Volksbad

Munich's most famous swimming pool (Map p108, B4; www.swm.de; Rosenheimer Strasse 1; adult/child €4.50/3.40; ⏲7.30am-11pm; 🚊Am Gasteig) is an exquisite art nouveau affair that first opened its doors in 1901. It's one of Europe's most attractive swimming baths and a dip here under the ornate stuccoed ceiling is a real treat. Despite the period look, it boasts 21st-century pool and sauna technology.

❸ Muffatwerk

The Biergarten Muffatwerk (p115) is a kind of cooler version of the traditional Munich beer garden: reggae instead of oompah, vegetarian plates instead of pig-knuckle platters. There's regular live music in the evenings and a great vibe all day long.

❹ Gasteig

You cannot fail to notice the Gasteig (p110), a mammoth building in brick and glass rising confidently over Am Gasteig and Rosenheimer Strasse. It's one of southern Germany's top concert venues attracting huge international acts. It's undergoing a major renovation.

❺ Herbergsmuseum & Kriechbaumhof

In Preysingstrasse, the Herbergsmuseum is a tiny former worker's cottage that has been done up as it would have been when it was inhabited by a labourer's family in the 19th century. Opposite, the conspicuous all-timber Kriechbaumhof looks like it's been teleported from the Alps.

❻ Haidhausen Cemetery

The austere, slender spire of the Church of John the Baptist rises above Kirchenstrasse and the adjoining and somewhat overgrown walled cemetery, one of Munich's most attractive, with rows of tombs in different artistic styles. Its most famous resident is Austrian actor Kurt Zips.

❼ Wiener Platz

So called as it marked the start of the road to Vienna, busy Wiener Platz is known for its daily gourmet market, which has been held since 1901 under a supersize maypole. Tiny cafes and kiosks sell everything from fish mains to chocolate to sausages, and it's a great place to lunch or snack.

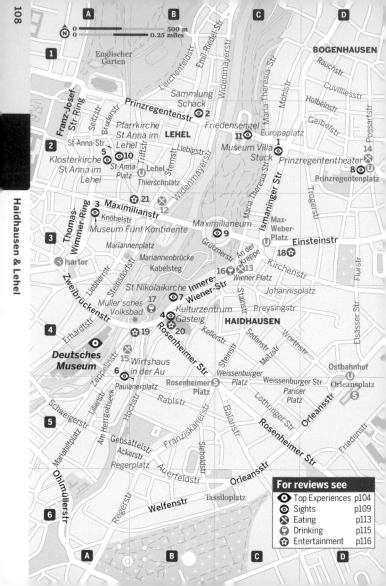

BOGENHAUSEN

Englischer Garten

0 ——— 500 m
0 ——— 0.25 miles

Sammlung Schack **2**

Prinzregentenstr

Friedensengel

LEHEL

Pfarrkirche St Anna im Lehel

11 Museum Villa Stuck **1**

14

Europaplatz

Prinzregententheater

Klosterkirche St Anna im Lehel **5** **10**

St-Anna-Platz

Lehel

Thierschplatz

8 Prinzregentenplatz

21 **3** Maximilianstr

Knöbelstr

Museum Fünf Kontinente

Maximilianeum **9**

Max-Weber-Platz

12

Mariannenplatz

Marianenbrücke

Kabelsteg

An der Kreppe

18

Einsteinstr

Kirchenstr

Isartor

St Nikolaikirche

16 **13** Wiener Platz

Innere-Wiener-Str

Johannisplatz

Müller'sches Volksbad **17**

7

Kulturzentrum Gasteig

Preysingstr

HAIDHAUSEN

4

20

19

15 Wirtshaus in der Au

6

Pauianerplatz

Rosenheimer Str

Deutsches Museum

Weissenburger Platz

Ostbahnhof

Orleansplatz

Rosenheimer Platz

Weissenburger Str

Pariser Platz

Orleansstr

Rablstr

Rosenheimer Str

Orleansstr

Welfenstr

Tassiloplatz

For reviews see	
⊙ Top Experiences	p104
⊙ Sights	p109
✕ Eating	p113
🍺 Drinking	p115
☆ Entertainment	p116

Sights

Museum Villa Stuck
MUSEUM

1 ◎ MAP P108, C2

Around the turn of the 20th century, Franz von Stuck was a leading light on Munich's art scene, and his residence is one of the finest *Jugendstil* homes you're ever likely to see. Stuck came up with the intricate design, which forges tapestries, patterned floors, coffered ceilings and other elements into a harmonious work of art. Today his glorious pad is open as a museum with changing exhibitions. (☏089-455 5510; www.villastuck.de; Prinzregentenstrasse 60; adult/concession €9/4.50; ⊙11am-6pm Tue-Sun; 🚋Friedensengel/Villa Stuck)

Friedensengel (p113)

Symphonie Orchestra

Charismatic Lithuanian maestro Mariss Jansons has rejuvenated the playlist of the **BR-Symphonieorchester** (☏089-590 001; www.br-so.com) and it often performs with its choir at such venues as the Gasteig (p110) and the Prinzregententheater (p112).

Sammlung Schack
MUSEUM

2 ◎ MAP P108, B2

Count Adolf Friedrich von Schack (1815–94) was a great fan of 19th-century Romantic painters such as Böcklin, Feuerbach and von Schwind. His collection is housed in the former Prussian embassy, now the Schack-Galerie. A tour of the intimate space is like an escape into the idealised fantasy worlds created by these artists. (www.sammlung-schack.de; Prinzregentenstrasse 9; adult/concession €4/3; ⊙10am-6pm Wed-Sun; 🚋Reitmorstrasse/Sammlung Schack)

Museum Fünf Kontinente
MUSEUM

3 ◎ MAP P108, A3

A bonanza of art and objects from Africa, India, the Americas, the Middle East and Polynesia, the State Museum of Ethnology has one of the most prestigious and complete ethnological collections anywhere. Sculpture from West and Central Africa is particularly impressive, as are Peruvian ceramics, Indian jewellery, mummy parts, and artefacts from the days of Captain Cook. (State Museum of Ethnology; www.museum-fuenf-kontinente.de; Maximilianstrasse 42; adult/child €5/free, Sun €1; ⏲9.30am-5.30pm Tue-Sun; 🚋Maxmonument)

Kulturzentrum Gasteig
CULTURAL CENTRE

4 ◉ MAP P108, B4

One of Munich's top cultural venues, the Kulturzentrum Gasteig caused quite a controversy in the mid-eighties due to its postmodern, boxy, glass-and-brick design in XXL dimensions. The complex

harbours four concert halls, including the 2400-seat Philharmonie, the home of the Münchner Philharmoniker. It also attracts some huge names in the world of popular music. While it's undergoing major renovations, performances will be at **Gasteig HP8** (Hans-Pressinger-Strasse 4–8, Sendling). (Gasteig Culture Centre; ☎tickets 089-548 181 81; www.gasteig.de; Rosenheimer Strasse 5; 🚋Am Gasteig)

Klosterkirche St Anna im Lehel
CHURCH

5 ◉ MAP P108, A2

The Asamkirche may be more sumptuous, but the Klosterkirche St Anna im Lehel is actually a collaboration of the top dogs of the rococo. Johann Michael

Klosterkirche St Anna im Lehel

Worth a Trip: Lake Starnberg

Around 25km southwest of Munich, glittering Lake Starnberg (Starnberger See) was once the haunt of Bavaria's royal family but now provides a bit of easily accessible R&R for anyone looking to escape the hustle of the Bavarian capital.

At the northern end of the lake, the affluent, century-old town of Starnberg is the northern gateway. The S-Bahn station is just steps from the lakeshore, where you'll find cruise-boat landing docks, pedal-boat hire and lots of strolling day-trippers.

An easy 5km hike along the shore takes you to Berg, where King Ludwig II spent summers at Schloss Berg and where he and his doctor died in 1886 under mysterious circumstances. The palace and its lovely gardens still belong to the Wittelsbach family and are closed to prying eyes, but you're free to walk through its wooded park to the Votivkapelle. Built in honour of Ludwig and shrouded by mature trees, this neo-Romanesque memorial chapel overlooks the spot in the lake – marked by a simple cross, erected years later by his mother – where Ludwig's dead body was supposedly found.

Lake Starnberg is just one of the lakes in the Fünf-Seen-Land. The others are Ammersee and the much smaller Pilsensee, Wörthsee and Wesslinger See.

Starnberg is a half-hour ride on the S6 train from Munich Hauptbahnhof (€5.80).

Fischer designed the building, and Cosmas Damian Asam painted the stunning ceiling fresco and altar. This was the first rococo church to be built in Munich. (St-Anna-Platz 21; ⊙6am-7pm; ⌷Lehel, Ⓤ Lehel)

Wirtshaus in der Au   COOKING

6 ◉ MAP P108, A4

Munich's king of *Knödel* (dumplings) since 1901 runs an English-language dumpling-making workshop. (☏089-448 14 00; www.wirtshausinderau.de; Lilienstrasse 51; ⌷Deutsches Museum)

St Nikolaikirche   CHURCH

7 ◉ MAP P108, B4

St Nikolaikirche was first built in 1315 in Gothic style, only to go all baroque three centuries later. Outside the prim church ensemble of St Nikolai and Lorettokapelle, the covered walkway protects some pretty nifty 'Stations of the Cross' made of Nymphenburg porcelain. Today the church is used by a Ukrainian Orthodox congregation. (St Nicholas Church; Innere-Wiener-Strasse; ⌷Am Gasteig)

Out & About in Munich

♁

Munich's gay and lesbian scene is the liveliest in Bavaria but tame compared to that of Berlin, Cologne or Amsterdam. The rainbow flag flies especially proudly along Müllerstrasse and the adjoining Glockenbachviertel and Gärtnerplatzviertel. To plug into the scene, keep an eye out for freebie mags *Our Munich* and *Sergej,* which contain up-to-date listings and news about the community and gay-friendly establishments around town. Another source of info is www.gaytouristoffice.com/en/home.

Sub (p148) is a one-stop service and information agency; lesbians can also turn to Le Tra (p149).

The main street parties of the year are **Christopher Street Day** (www.csd-munich.de), held on Marienplatz on the second weekend in July, and the **Hans Sachs Strassenfest** (www.hans-sachs-strassenfest.de), held in mid-August along Hans-Sachs-Strasse in the Glockenbachviertel. During Oktoberfest, LGBTIQ+ folks take over the Bräurosl beer tent on the first Sunday and Fischer-Vroni on the second Monday.

Prinzregententheater THEATRE

8 ◉ MAP P108, D2

One of Bogenhausen's main landmarks is the Prinzregententheater. Its dramatic mix of art nouveau and neoclassical styles was conceived under Prince Regent Luitpold as a festival house for Richard Wagner operas. (📞089-218 502; www.theaterakademie.de; Prinzregentenplatz 12; ⓢ Prinzregentenplatz)

Maximilianeum HISTORIC BUILDING

9 ◉ MAP P108, C3

Maximilianstrasse culminates in the glorious Maximilianeum, completed in 1874, a decade after Maximilian II's sudden death. It's an imposing structure, drawn like

a theatre curtain across a hilltop, bedecked with mosaics, paintings and other artistic objects. It's framed by an undulating park called the Maximiliananlagen, which is a haven for cyclists in summer and tobogganists in winter. (Max-Planck-Strasse 1; 🚊Maximilianeum)

Pfarrkirche St Anna im Lehel CHURCH

10 ◉ MAP P108, A2

The rather pompous neo-Romanesque Pfarrkirche St Anna im Lehel arrived on the scene in 1892 when the Klosterkirche St Anna im Lehel became too small. Conceived by locally born architect Gabriel von Seidl, it's worth a spin for the huge Byzantine-style painting behind the altar and little art nouveau touches throughout. (St-Anna-Platz 5; ⊘8am-5pm Mon-Sat, to 8pm Sun; 🚊Lehel, Ⓢ Lehel)

Friedensengel

STATUE

11 ◉ MAP P108, C2

Just east of the Isar River, the Friedensengel (Angel of Peace) statue stands guard from its perch atop a 23m-high column. It commemorates the 1871 Treaty of Versailles, which ended the Franco-Prussian War, and the base contains some shimmering golden Roman-style mosaics. (Prinzregentenstrasse; 🚊Friedensengel/Villa Stuck)

Eating

Wirtshaus in der Au

BAVARIAN €€

The slogan of this Bavarian tavern (see **6** ◉ Map p108, A4) is 'Beer and dumplings since 1901', and it's this time-honoured staple – dumplings – that's the speciality here (the tavern even runs a dumpling-making course in English). Once a brewery, the space-rich dining area has chunky tiled floors, a lofty ceiling and a crackling fireplace in winter. When spring springs, the beer garden fills. (📞089-448 1400; www.wirtshausinderau.de; Lilienstrasse 51; mains €10-22; ⊘5pm-midnight Mon-Fri, from 10am Sat & Sun; 🚊Deutsches Museum)

Maximilianeum

Sir Tobi

BAVARIAN €€

12 MAP P108, B3

This Bavarian bistro serves delicious, slow-food versions of southern German and Austrian dishes in an environment of crisp white tablecloths and fresh flowers. The service here is particularly good. (089-3249 4825; www.sirtobi-muenchen.de; Sternstrasse 16; mains €9-20; 11.30am-3pm Mon-Fri, 5.30pm-midnight Thu-Sat; Lehel)

Fischhäusl

SEAFOOD €€

13 MAP P108, C3

Part of the food market on Wiener Platz, this kiosk with a few seats is one of the best spots in Munich to lunch on fish, which is prepared simply on a grill and served with salad, potatoes and white wine. (Wiener Platz; mains €7-15; 9.30am-6pm Tue-Fri, 9am-2.30pm Sat; Wiener Platz)

Swagat

INDIAN €€

14 MAP P108, D2

Swagat fills every nook of an intimate cellar space with Indian fabrics, cavorting Hindu gods and snow-white tablecloths. The curry is as hot as Bavarians can take it, and there's plenty to please non-carnivores. (Prinzregentenplatz 13; mains €10.50-22.50; 11.30am-2.30pm & 5.30pm-1am; Prinzregentenplatz, Prinzregentenplatz)

Wiener Platz (p107)

FOOTTOO/GETTY IMAGES ©

Showroom

GASTRONOMY €€€

15 MAP P108, A4

Andreas Schweiger's crossover creations strike just the right balance between adventure and comfort, which is why his Michelin-starred restaurant is among the most respected in town. The finely crafted dishes on offer are beyond the means of most mortals, so this is definitely one for very special occasions. (089-4442 9082; Lilienstrasse 6; 5-course menu €115-135; 6pm-1am Mon-Fri; Deutsches Museum)

Drinking

Hofbräukeller

BEER HALL

16 MAP P108, C3

One of Munich's original beer halls, this wood-panelled, staunchly traditional tavern serves nine different types of the finest Hofbräu, including two alcohol-free versions and always a seasonal brew. Out the back is what was, many claim, Munich's very first beer garden. (089-459 9250; www.hofbraeukeller.de; Wiener Platz; 10am-midnight; Wiener Platz)

Biergarten Muffatwerk

BEER GARDEN

17 MAP P108, B4

Think of this one as a progressive beer garden with reggae instead of

Best Munich Blogs

My Adventures in Munich (www.myadventuresinmunich.blogspot.com) Trials and tribulations of an expat in Munich.

Arts in Munich (www.artsinmunich.com) Covers culture, art, eating and wellness in the Bavarian capital and beyond.

Elsewhere and Here (www.elsewhereandhere.com) City tips from author and guide Monika Pfundmeier.

Around About Munich (www.aroundaboutmunich.de) Free-time family tips for the Munich area.

Move to Munich (www.movetomunich.com) Interesting blog on relocating and living in Munich.

oompah, civilised imbibing instead of brainless guzzling, organic meats, fish and vegetables on the grill, and the option of chilling in lounge chairs. Opening hours are open-ended, meaning some very late finishes. (www.muffatwerk.de; Zellstrasse 4; from noon mid-Mar–mid-Oct; Am Gasteig)

Entertainment

Jazzclub Unterfahrt im Einstein
LIVE MUSIC

18 ⭐ MAP P108, C3

Join a diverse crowd at this long-established, intimate club for a mixed bag of acts ranging from old bebop to edgy experimental. The Sunday open-jam session is legendary. (☎089-448 2794; www.unterfahrt.de; Einsteinstrasse 42; ⏰from 9pm; Ⓤ Max-Weber-Platz)

Museum-Lichtspiele
CINEMA

19 ⭐ MAP P108, B4

Cult cinema with wacky interior and screenings of the *Rocky Horror Picture Show* (11.10pm Friday and Saturday nights).

Shows English-language movies. (☎089-482 403; www.museum-lichtspiele.de; Lilienstrasse 2; 🚇 Deutsches Museum)

Münchner Philharmoniker
CLASSICAL MUSIC

20 ⭐ MAP P108, B4

Munich's premier orchestra normally performs at the Gasteig Cultural Centre (p110). While the Gasteig is being renovated, performances will be at its new home, the Isarphilharmonie, one of the buildings at Gasteig HP8.

Book tickets early, as these performances usually sell out. (☎089-480 985 500; www.mphil.de; Hans-Preissinger-Strasse 8; ⏰mid-Sep–Jun; 🚋 Brudermühlstrasse)

Pretzels and Munich's Paulaner beer

MARADON 333/SHUTTERSTOCK ©

Strong Beer Time

The 'Strong Beer Time' originally developed to make the fasting season of Lent more bearable. It's thought monks brewed more potent beer at this time to make up for the meagre rations they consumed, and the locals were more than willing to join them.

Today the Starkbierzeit has turned into another mini-Oktoberfest (for beer fans it conveniently falls between Oktoberfest and the opening of the city's beer gardens), celebrated with beverages containing almost 8% alcohol. The most famous of these is Salvator, pumped with abandon by the Paulaner brewery.

To join in the inebriated revelry of the Starkbierzeit, head to the Augustinerkeller, Nockherberg and the Löwenbräukeller.

GOP Varieté Theater

THEATRE

21 ⭐ MAP P108, B3

Hosts a real jumble of acts and shows, from magicians to light comedies to musicals. (📞089-210 288 444; www.variete.de; Maximilianstrasse 47; 🚋Maxmonument)

Explore ✪

Nymphenburg, BMW & Olympiapark

Occupying a huge swath of northwest Munich, the neighbourhoods of Nymphenburg, Neuhausen and the Olympiapark are a varied trio. The Olympiapark is mostly about one thing – the venues left over from the 1972 summer games. Nymphenburg is all about its royal palace, Munich's finest, while little-visited and mostly residential Neuhausen has Europe's largest beer garden.

Visits to this part of Munich revolve around three big sights - Schloss Nymphenburg (p120), the Olympiapark (p122) and BMW World & Museum (p124). If you want to see all three in a day, you'd better start early at the Olympiapark, perhaps taking the earliest tour and enjoying a flying visit to the Olympiaturm before heading to BMW. From there make your way to Nymphenburg for a tour of the Schloss and a wander in the grounds – end the day at Munich's largest beer garden, the Hirschgarten (p136) where you can join 7999 other drinkers for a stein of Augustiner.

Getting There & Around

U The best stop for the Olympiapark and BMW is Petuelring served by the U3. One stop further north is Olympiazentrum.

🚊 The only way to reach Nymphenburg by public transport is aboard tram 17.

Neighbourhood Map on p128

Olympiaturm (p123), Olympiapark PHILLUS/SHUTTERSTOCK ©

Top Experience 📷
Admire Schloss Nymphenburg's Women's Portraits

This palace and its delightful gardens sprawl around 5km northwest of Altstadt. Begun in 1664 as a villa for Electress Adelaide of Savoy, it was extended over the next century to create the royal family's summer residence. Franz, Duke of Bavaria, head of the once royal Wittelsbach family, still occupies an apartment here. The highlight is the Schönheitengalerie of 19th-century beauties.

◎ MAP P128, B4

www.schloss-nymphen burg.de

castle adult/child €6/free, all sites €11.50/free

⏱9am-6pm Apr–mid-Oct, 10am-4pm mid-Oct–Mar

🚋Schloss Nymphenburg

Main Building

The main palace building consists of a large villa and two wings of creaking parquet floors and sumptuous period rooms. At the beginning of the self-guided tour comes the high point of the entire Schloss, the **Schönheitengalerie**, housed in the former apartments of Queen Caroline. Some 38 portraits of women, chosen by an admiring King Ludwig I, peer from the walls. The most famous image is of Helene Sedlmayr, the daughter of a shoemaker, wearing a lavish frock the king gave her for the sitting. You'll also find Ludwig's beautiful, and notorious, lover Lola Montez.

Further along the tour route comes the **Queen's Bedroom**, which still contains the sleigh bed on which Ludwig II was born, and the **King's Chamber**, resplendent with three-dimensional ceiling frescoes.

Marstallmuseum

Also in the main building is the **Marstallmuseum** (adult/child €4.50/free), displaying royal coaches and riding gear. This includes Ludwig II's fairy tale–like rococo sleigh, ingeniously fitted with oil lamps for his crazed nocturnal outings. Upstairs is the world's largest collection of porcelain made by the famous Nymphenburger Manufaktur. Also known as the Sammlung Bäuml, it presents the entire product palette from the company's founding in 1747 until 1930.

Palace Grounds

Behind the palace is a sprawling park where you'll find several follies. The chief attraction, the **Amalienburg**, is a small hunting lodge dripping with crystal and gilt decoration; don't miss the amazing hall of mirrors. The two-storey **Pagodenburg** was built in the early 18th century as a Chinese teahouse. The **Badenburg** is a sauna and bathing house that still has its original heating system. Finally, the **Magdalenenklause** was built as a mock hermitage in faux-ruined style.

★ Top Tips

o From October to March admission is reduced as some of the outbuildings and follies are closed.

o Under-18s get in free of charge.

o Nymphenburg is undergoing constant renovation and some parts may be closed when you visit.

o The palace hosts top-quality chamber-music concerts – see the website for details.

✗ Take a Break

In the grounds, the Schlosscafé im Palmenhaus (p135) serves light lunches.

At the end of the day, head to Hirschgarten (p136), south of Nymphenburg, Bavaria's largest beer garden.

Top Experience 📷
Relive Germany's FIFA World Cup Victory at Olympiapark

The area to the north of the city, where soldiers once paraded and the world's first Zeppelin landed in 1909, found a new role in the '60s as the Olympiapark. Built for the '72 Olympic Games, it has a small-scale feel, and some may be amazed that the games could once have been held at such a modest venue. The 85-hectare site is dotted with attractions – allow a day to see everything.

◎ MAP P128, H1

Olympic Park

www.olympiapark.de

stadium tour adult/
concession €8/6

🕑 stadium tours 11am,
1pm & 4pm Apr-Oct

Ⓤ Olympiazentrum

Info-Pavillion

A good first stop is the Info-Pavilion at the Olympia-Eissportzentrum (p132), which has information, maps, tour tickets and a model of the complex. There is an app for a self-guided audio tour in German or English.

Olympiastadion

Germans have a soft spot for the **Olympiastadion** (Olympic Stadium; ☉9am-8pm mid-May–mid-Sep, shorter hr rest of yr) because it was on this hallowed grass in 1974 that the national soccer team – led by the Kaiser, Franz Beckenbauer – won the FIFA World Cup. The stadium was once home to local team Bayern Munich before they moved to the Allianz Arena in 2006, so it will be instantly recognisable to soccer fans, with its contorted steel and Plexiglas tent roof, which stretches across the stands, though not the pitch. Amazingly, you can take a stroll on the roof (p130).

Olympiaturm

When the sky is clear, you'll have Munich at your feet against the breathtaking backdrop of the Alps from the top of the 290m **Olympiaturm** (Olympic Tower; ☎089-3067 2750; www.olympiapark.de; adult/child €11/7; ☉9am-midnight; Ⓤ Olympiazentrum). It's one of the top attractions in the Olympiapark.

Monument

In 2017 a monument (p127) to the Israeli athletes and West German police killed in the Olympic hostage situation was finally unveiled. Visit the monument to learn about this grim side to the 1972 games (p131).

★ **Top Tips**

o A good first stop is the Info-Pavilion, which has information, maps, tour tickets and self-guided audio tour players.

o The Olympia-Eissportzentrum and Olympia Schwimmhalle are Olympic venues you can actually still do sport in.

✕ **Take a Break**

There are plenty of chain restaurants and other eateries within the park.

Top Experience 📷
See How BMWs Are Made

As any true petrolhead will tell you, BMW cars are made in Munich, where the company has had its headquarters from the very beginning. To the west of the Olympiapark, you'll find three blockbuster BMW sights – BMW World, the BMW Museum and the BMW plant itself. All three can be managed in a day, but only in 5th gear. BMW World is also home to the city's best fine-dining restaurant.

◎ MAP P128, H1

📞 089-125 016 001

www.bmw-welt.de

Am Olympiapark 1

tours adult/child €7/5

🕐 7.30am-midnight Mon-Sat, from 9am Sun

Ⓤ Olympiazentrum

BMW Welt

Next to the Olympiapark, the glass-and-steel, double-cone tornado spiralling down from a dark cloud the size of an aircraft carrier holds BMW Welt, truly a petrolhead's dream. Apart from its role as a prestigious car pick-up centre, this king of showrooms acts as a shop window for BMW's latest models and a show space for the company in general.

Straddle a powerful motorbike, marvel at technology-packed saloons and estates or take the 80-minute guided tour. On the Junior Campus, kids learn about mobility, fancy themselves car engineers and even get to design their own vehicle in workshops. Hang around long enough and you're sure to see motorbike stunts on the staircases and other petroleum-fuelled antics.

BMW Museum

This silver, bowl-shaped **museum** (adult/child €10/7; ⏱10am-6pm Tue-Sun) comprises seven themed 'houses', which examine the development of BMW's product line and include sections on motorcycles and motor racing. The interior design – with its curvy retro feel, futuristic bridges, squares and huge backlit wall screens – is reason enough to visit.

BMW Plant

If you like cars, be sure not to miss a fascinating tour of BMW's state-of-the-art plant. The tours (p130), in English and German, last 2½ hours and take in the entire production process. Around 950 cars and 3000 engines are produced here daily. Booking well ahead is essential, especially in summer.

Esszimmer

BMW World's house restaurant, Esszimmer (p135), quickly established itself at the top table of Munich's foodie scene.

★ Top Tips

o Check the BMW Welt website for other tours of other locations, such as the company's recycling and dismantling centre.

o BMW Museum tickets are valid for five hours after validation.

o The BMW World store is one of the best shops for kids in Munich.

✗ Take a Break

BMW World has a fairly reasonably priced cafe – otherwise bring a picnic to enjoy on the grass in the Olympiapark.

Walking Tour 🥾

Lesser-Known Olympiapark

Around 5km northwest of Marienplatz lies the huge Olympiapark, venue for the 1974 Summer Olympic Games. Unlike some notorious cases, Munich didn't leave its Olympic venues to rot once the last race had been run. In fact, there are some well-known attractions here. That said, there are also some little-visited places around the park with interesting stories to tell.

Walk Facts

Start Flohmarkt Olympia-park; 🚈 Olympiapark West

End Erinnerungsort Olympia-Atentat; Ⓤ Olympiazentrum

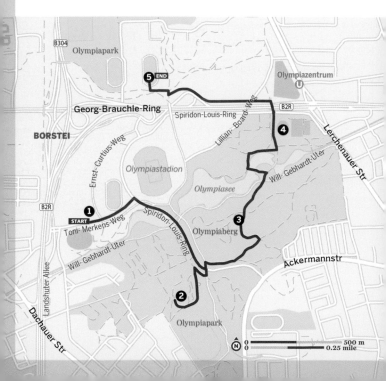

❶ Flohmarkt Olympiapark

What does every German city do with its spare bits of land – why hold a flea market on them, of course! The jumble sale (p136) at the Olympiapark takes place near the Olympiastadion almost every Friday and Saturday from 7am until 4pm.

❷ Ost-West Friedenskirche

The East-West Peace Church (p130) is one of the very few structures within the Olympiapark that predate the Olympics. This Russian Orthodox church was built illegally by a Russian hermit after WWII and narrowly avoided being demolished for the games. The hermit's house was turned into a museum in 2004. The church really wouldn't look out of place in rural Siberia.

❸ Olympiaberg

The **Olympic Mountain** is one of the highest points in Munich and thus offers sweeping views of the Olympiapark, the city and even the Alps when conditions are right. It was artificially created using rubble from WWII bomb sites and actually stood here long before the Olympiapark arrived. In winter it's a popular skiing and sledging spot.

❹ Walk of Stars

Imitating a Holywood-style Walk of Fame, the Olympiapark's Walk of Stars is a series of concrete tablets with handprints and footprints left behind by famous people. Illustrious celebrities to have left their mark include David Copperfield, Jon Bon Jovi and Cliff Richard.

❺ Erinnerungsort Olympia-Atentat

Sadly the 1972 Munich Olympics are known for the hostage taking of Israeli athletes by Palestinian terrorists. Eleven Olympians died and this **monument** (Kolehmainenweg, Olympiapark; admission free; ⏱8am-10pm; Ⓤ Olympiazentrum), finally opened in 2017, remembers them and the events of those terrible days.

For reviews see

👁	Top Experiences	p120
◉	Sights	p130
✕	Eating	p133
🍷	Drinking	p136
★	Entertainment	p136
🔒	Shopping	p136

0   1 km
0   0.5 mile

MOOSACH

Westfriedho

Westfriedhof

GERN

Hugo-Troendle-Str

Allacher Str

Tent

In den Kirschen

Wintrichring

Baldurstr

Nederlinger Str

NEULUSTHEIM

Neuer Botanischer Garten ◉9

Schlosspark

Museum Mensch und Natur 🔒20

Menzingerstr

Zamboninistr

Tizianstr

Südliche Auffahrtsallee

Notburgastr

Washington-Str

Prinzenstr

Lachnerstr

✕13

◉ **Schloss Nymphenburg**

NYMPHENBURG

Romanstr

Laimer Str

Wotanstr

Wendl-Dietrich-Str

Wotanstr

De-La-Paz-Str

Königbauerstr

Wilhelm-Hale-Str

Arnulfstr

🍷16

17

🔒

Laim

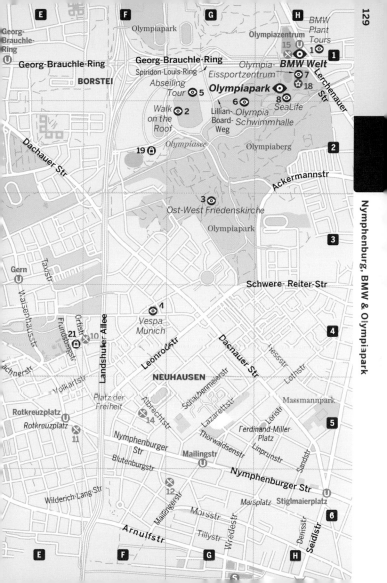

Sights

BMW Plant Tours   TOURS

1 👁 MAP P128, H1

If you like cars, don't miss a tour of BMW's state-of-the-art plant. The tours in English and German last 2½ hours and take in the entire production process. Booking well ahead is essential, especially in summer. (☏089-125 016 001; www. bmw-welt.com; adult/child €9/6; ⊘in English 11.30am & 2pm Mon-Fri, in German 6pm; Ⓤ Petuelring)

Walk on the Roof   WALKING

2 👁 MAP P128, G2

Can't make it to the Alps for a high-altitude clamber? No matter. Just head to the Olympic Stadium for a walk on the roof. Yup, the roof; that famously contorted steel and Plexiglas confection is ready for its close-up. Just like in the mountains, you'll be roped and hooked up to a steel cable as you clamber around under the eagle-eyed supervision of an experienced guide showering you with fascinating details about the stadium's architecture and construction. (adult/concessions €43/33; ⊘2.30pm Apr-Oct)

Ost-West Friedenskirche   CHURCH

3 👁 MAP P128, G3

Built illegally after WWII by a Russian hermit called Father Timofey, the delightfully rural Russian Orthodox East-West Peace Church was to have been demolished for the Olympic Games of 1972 but

Olympiastadion roof

The Games Must Go On

The 1972 Summer Olympics were particularly significant for Munich as they gave the city a chance to make a historic break with the past. It was the first time the country would host the prestigious sporting event since 1936, when the games were held in Berlin under Hitler. The motto was the 'Happy Games', and the emblem was a blue sun spiral. The city built an innovative Olympic Park, which included tent-like plexiglass canopies that were revolutionary for the times. It was the perfect opportunity to present a new, democratic Germany full of pride and optimism.

But in the final week of the games disaster struck. Members of a Palestinian terrorist group known as 'Black September' killed two Israeli athletes and took nine others hostage at the Olympic Village, demanding the release of political prisoners and an escape aircraft. During a failed rescue attempt by German security forces at Fürstenfeldbruck, a military base west of Munich, all of the hostages and most of the terrorists were killed. Competition was suspended briefly before Avery Brundage, the International Olympic Committee president, famously declared 'the Games must go on'. The bloody incident cast a pall over the entire Olympics and over sporting events in Germany for years to follow.

These tragic events are chronicled in an Oscar-winning documentary, *One Day in September* (1999) by Kevin McDonald, as well as in Steven Spielberg's historical-fictional account, *Munich* (2005). However it took until 2017 for a monument to those killed to be unveiled in Munich. It stands north of the Olympic Stadium and includes a video on a loop about the tragic events of 1972.

protests led to the repositioning of some of the venues further north. When Timofey died in 2004, his adjacent house was made into a museum. The buildings are two of only a handful of structures within the Olympiapark that predate the games. (East-West Peace Church; www.ost-west-friedenskirche.de; Spiridon-Louis Ring 100, Olympiapark-süd; admission free; 🚇Goethe-Institut)

Vespa Munich

TOURS

4 ◉ MAP P128, F4

Book in advance, pick up your vespa and spend the day bombing around Munich guided by the GPS unit provided. It's the latest fun way to see the city, but good luck on those freeways! (☎0151-517 251 69; www.vespamunich.com; Dom Pedro-Strasse 26; full-day tour €59;

Museum of Humankind & Nature

Nothing to do with the royal grandeur of Schloss Nymphenburg, kids will have plenty of ooh and aah moments in the **Museum Mensch und Natur** (Museum of Humankind & Nature; Map p128, B4; www.mmn-muenchen.de; Schloss Nymphenburg; adult/child €3.50/2.50; ☺9am-5pm Tue, Wed & Fri, to 8pm Thu, 10am-6pm Sat & Sun; 🚋Schloss Nymphenburg), in the palace's north wing. Anything but old school, it puts a premium on interactive displays, models, audiovisual presentations and attractive animal dioramas. It's all in German, but few language skills are needed to appreciate the visuals.

☺office 10am-2pm daily, pick-ups 9am-6pm; 🚋Leonrodplatz)

Abseiling Tour ADVENTURE

5 ◉ MAP P128, G1

True daredevils might be tempted by this abseiling tour, which has you scaling up the Olympiastadion's north side to a height of 40m, then heading straight back down in a free rappel. (www.olympiapark.de; adult/concession €53/43; ☺5pm May-Oct)

Olympia Schwimmhalle SWIMMING

6 ◉ MAP P128, G2

The indoor Olympia Schwimmhalle was completely renovated in 2018 and is now the most modern and well-equipped swimming complex in Munich. (www.swm.de; Coubertinplatz 1; 3hr pass adult/child €4.80/3.80; ☺10am-7pm Mon, to 10pm Tue-Sun; 🆂Olympiazentrum)

Olympia-Eissportzentrum ICE SKATING

7 ◉ MAP P128, H1

Ice-skaters can glide alongside future medallists in the Olympia-Eissportzentrum. There's skate hire available for those who don't have their own. (📞089-306 70; www.olympiapark.de; Spiridon-Louis-Ring 21; adult/child per session €4.50/3; ☺check website for times)

SeaLife AQUARIUM

8 ◉ MAP P128, H1

If you're looking to keep the kids amused, SeaLife is the place to head. Reef sharks, moray eels and seahorses are among the 10,000 creatures on display, all presented in aquariums with recessed glass viewing ports. Tunnel walkways lead you right through some tanks – the next best thing to scuba diving. Save money by purchasing tickets online beforehand. (www.visitsealife.

com; Willi-Daume-Platz 1; adult/child gate prices €17.95/14.50; ⏱10am-5pm Mon-Fri, to 6pm Sat & Sun; Ⓢ Olympiazentrum)

Neuer Botanischer Garten

GARDENS

9 ◎ MAP P128, A4

Munich's verdant New Botanical Garden segues smoothly from the north side of the palace park and ranks among the most important in Europe. About a century old, it boasts some 14,000 plant species from around the world. Highlights include the Victorian-style *Palmenhaus* (glass palm house) with its famous collection of tropical and subtropical plants. Other greenhouses shelter cacti, orchids, ferns, carnivorous plants and other leafy treasures. (New Botanical Garden; www.botmuc.de; Menzinger Strasse 65; adult/child €4.50/3, Palmenhaus audioguide €3; ⏱9am-7pm May-Aug, to 6pm Apr & Sep, to 5pm Feb-Mar & Oct, to 4.30pm Nov-Jan; 🚋 Schloss Nymphenburg)

Eating

Ruffini

CAFE €

10 ✗ MAP P128, F4

Well worth the effort of delving deep into Neuhausen to find it, this cafe is a fun place to be no matter where the hands of the clock are. On sunny days the self-service rooftop terrace gets busy with locals – few tourists make

Olympia Schwimmhalle

Bavaria Filmstadt

Movie magic is the draw of the **Bavaria Filmstadt** (☎089-6499 2000; www.filmstadt.de; Bavariafilmplatz 7; all attractions adult/child €27.50/22; �9am-6pm; ⓡBavariafilmplatz), a theme park built around Bavaria Film, one of Germany's oldest studios, founded in 1919. The top-grossing German film of all time, Das Boot, was among the classics shot here, though now the studios focus more on TV production.

Films and TV are still produced today, and who knows, you might see a star during the guided 90-minute tours. The 1pm tour is in English.

The crash-and-burn Stunt Show is a runaway hit as well, while kids are particularly fond of the wacky 4D cinema, with seats that lurch, among other special effects from silly to spooky. The Filmstadt is in the southern suburb of Geiselgasteig, about 14km from the Altstadt. Take the U1 to Wettersteinplatz, then tram 25 to Bavariafilmplatz.

it out here. Hosts regular music events, from rock to classical. (www.ruffini.de; Orffstrasse 22; meals €7-10; �10am-midnight Tue-Sun; ⓡ; ⓡNeuhausen)

Eiscafé Sarcletti
GELATO €

11 ✖ MAP P128, E5

Ice-cream addicts have been getting their gelato fix at this Munich institution since 1879. Choose from more than 50 mouth-watering flavours, from not-so-plain vanilla to buttermilk and mango. (www.sarcletti.de; Nymphenburger Strasse 155; �9am-11.30pm May-Aug, shorter hours Sep-Apr; ⓤRotkreuzplatz)

Chopan
AFGHANI €€

12 ✖ MAP P128, G6

Munich has a huge Afghan community, the most respected eatery of which is this much-lauded restaurant done out in the style of a Central Asian caravanserai, with rich fabrics, multihued glass lanterns and geometric patterns. In this culinary Aladdin's cave, you'll discover a menu of lamb, lentils, rice, spinach and flatbread in various combinations. No alcohol. (☎089-1895 6459; www.chopan. de; Elvirastrasse 18a; mains €8-20; �6pm-midnight; ⓤMaillingerstrasse)

Schlosscafé im Palmenhaus

CAFE €€

13 ✕ MAP P128, A4

The glass-fronted 1820 palm house where Ludwig II used to keep his exotic house plants warm in winter is now a high-ceilinged and pleasantly scented cafe serving soups, salads, sandwiches and other light meals. It's just behind Schloss Nymphenburg. (☎089-175 309; www.palmenhaus.de; Schloss Nymphenburg 43; mains €10-17; ⏱11am-6pm Tue-Fri, from 10am Sat & Sun; ◻Schloss Nymphenburg)

Zauberberg

INTERNATIONAL €€

14 ✕ MAP P128, F5

Far off the tourist track, this 40-seat locals' favourite will put your tummy into a state of contentment with its elegant, well-composed international creations. Single plates are available, but in order to truly sample the chef's talents, you should order a multicourse menu. (Hedwigstrasse 14; 3-course dinner menu around €45; ⏱6.30pm-1am Tue-Sat; ◻Albrechtstrasse)

Esszimmer

MEDITERRANEAN €€€

15 ✕ MAP P128, H1

It took Bobby Bräuer, head chef at the gourmet restaurant at BMW World, just two years to gain his first Michelin star. Munich's top dining spot is the place to sample high-octane French and Mediterranean morsels, served in a trendy dark and veneered dining room above the i8s and 7

Hirschgarten (p136)

Series. Life in the gastronomic fast lane. (☎089-358 991 814; www.bmw-welt.com; BMW Welt, Am Olympiapark 1; 4/5 courses €130/145; ⏰from 7pm Tue-Sat; ❄ 📶; U Olympiazentrum)

Drinking

Hirschgarten

BEER GARDEN

16 MAP P128, B6

The Everest of Munich beer gardens can seat up to 8000 Augustiner lovers, making it Bavaria's biggest – an accolade indeed. It's in a lovely spot in a former royal hunting preserve and rubs up against a deer enclosure and a carousel. Steer here after visiting Schloss Nymphenburg – it's only a short walk south of the palace. (www.hirschgarten.de; Hirschgarten 1; ⏰11.30am-1am; 🚊Kriemhildenstrasse, S Laim)

Backstage

CLUB

17 MAP P128, D6

Refreshingly nonmainstream, this groovetastic club has a chilled night beer garden and a shape-shifting line-up of punk, nu metal, hip-hop, dance hall and other alternative sounds, both canned and live. (www.backstage.eu; Reitknechtstrasse 6; S Hirschgarten)

Entertainment

EHC München

ICE HOCKEY

18 MAP P128, H1

It's not one of Germany's premier ice-hockey outfits, but EHC München's games at the Olympic ice rink are exciting spectacles nonetheless; the team features several Canadian and American players. (www.ehc-muenchen.de; Olympia Eishalle, Olympiapark; U Olympiazentrum)

Shopping

Flohmarkt im Olympiapark

MARKET

19 MAP P128, F2

This large flea market, located outside the Olympiastadion,

Campground Accommodation

A kilometre north of Schloss Nymphenburg, the **Tent** (Map p128, A2; ☎089-141 4300; www.the-tent.com; In den Kirschen 30; tent bunks/fl space €12.50/9, campsites from €9; ⏰early Jun-end Oktoberfest; 📶; 🚊Botanischer Garten) is a youth-oriented camping ground with classic tent pitches as well as a 160-bunk main tent with floor space and foam mats for shoestring nomads. It's by far the cheapest sleep in town during the Oktoberfest.

is held on most Fridays and Saturdays. (Olympiapark; ⊙7am-4pm Fri & Sat; 🚇Olympiapark West)

Porzellan Manufaktur Nymphenburg

CERAMICS

20 🔒 MAP P128, B4

Traditional and contemporary fine porcelain masterpieces, created by the royal manufacturer. Prices of the works are high. (📞089-1791 970; www.nymphenburg. com; Nördliches Schlossrondell 8; ⊙10am-5pm Mon-Fri; 🚇Schloss Nymphenburg)

Brauseschwein

TOYS

21 🔒 MAP P128, E4

This wacky toy store sells everything from penny candy to joke articles

Beer Garden

One of Munich's nicest beer-garden oases, the **Waldwirtschaft Grosshesselohe** (📞089-7499 4030; www.waldwirtschaft.de; Georg-Kalb-Strasse 3; ⊙10am-10.30pm; 👪; 🚊Grosshesselohe/Isartalbahnhof) pumps Spaten beer to 2500 drinkers under shady chestnuts. There are idyllic views of the Isar valley and live jazz nightly in good weather from Easter through September. Kids can run amok in the big playground.

and wooden trains. (Frundsbergstrasse 52; ⊙10am-1pm & 3pm-6.30pm Mon-Fri, 11am-2pm Sat; 🚇Neuhausen)

Top Experience 📷
Raise a *Mass* (or Two) at Oktoberfest

The world's largest drink-a-thon and the traditional highlight of Bavaria's annual events calender, Oktoberfest is one of the best-known fairs on earth. No other event manages to mix such a level of crimson-faced humour, drunken debauchery and excessive consumption of beer with so much tradition, history and oompah music.

www.oktoberfest.de

🕐 mid-Sep-early Oct

Then & Now

Before it was the world's biggest collective booze-up, Oktoberfest was just organised as an elaborate wedding toast. In October 1810 the future king, Bavarian Crown Prince Ludwig I, married Princess Therese, and the newlyweds threw an enormous party at the city gates, complete with a horse race. The next year Ludwig's fun-loving subjects came back for more. The festival was extended and, to fend off autumn, was moved forward to September. As the years rolled on, the racehorses were dropped and sometimes the party had to be cancelled, but the institution called Oktoberfest was here to stay.

Nearly two centuries later, this 16-day extravaganza draws more than six million visitors a year to celebrate a marriage of good cheer and outright debauchery. A special dark, strong beer (Wies'nbier) is brewed for the occasion, and Müncheners spend the day at the office in Lederhosen and Dirndl in order to hit the festival right after work.

It's Tapped!

Starting at 10.45am on the first day, the brewer's parade (Festzug) travels through the city centre from the River Isar to the fairgrounds. At the Wies'n, focus switches to the Schottenhamel beer tent and the mayor of Munich who, on the stroke of noon, takes a mallet and knocks the tap into the first keg. *'Ozapft ist's!'* (literally 'It's tapped' in Bavarian dialect) he cries and Oktoberfest has begun. The next day resembles the opening of the Olympics, as a young woman on horseback leads a parade of costumed participants from all over the world.

★ Getting There

The nearest metro station to the Oktoberfest venue, the Wies'n, is called Theresienwiese or walk from the Hauptbahnhof.

★ Top Tips

o No cash changes hands within the beer tents – buy special metal tokens (*Biermarken*) from outside the tents.

o No admission fee is charged, but most of the fun costs something.

o Food at Oktoberfest is as pricey as the beer, so bring your own snacks.

o Tents are no-smoking only.

o If you pop out of a beer tent during the busy times, don't expect your seat to be free when you return.

o Last call for drinks is usually at 10.30pm.

o The Wies'n has its own post office, left-luggage office and childcare centre.

The Beer

Let's get down to the real reason most come to Oktoberfest – the beer. All the suds pulled at Oktoberfest must have been brewed in Munich, restricting the number of breweries to six: Hofbräu-München (of Hofbräuhaus fame), the world-famous Paulaner, Löwenbräu, Augustiner, and the less well-known Hacker-Pschorr and Spatenbräu. The famous 1L *Mass* brought to your table by a Dirndl-wearing waitress, contains pretty strong stuff as the breweries cook up special concoctions (*Oktoberfestbier*) for the occasion.

The Venue

The huge **Theresienwiese** (Theresa Meadow; U Theresienwiese), better known as Wies'n, southwest of the Altstadt, is the site of the Oktoberfest. At the western end of the 'meadow' is the **Ruhmeshalle** (Hall of Fame; Theresienhöhe 16; admission free), an open gallery of famous Bavarians, whose busts adorn the wall like hunting trophies. The hall curls horseshoe-like around the **Bavariastatue** (Statue of Bavaria; Theresienhöhe 16; adult/child €3.50/2.50; ⊙9am-6pm Apr–mid-Oct, to 8pm during Oktoberfest), an 18m-high Amazon in the Statue of Liberty tradition, oak wreath in her hand and lion at her feet.

This iron lady has a cunning design that makes her seem solid, but actually you can climb via the knee joint up to the head for a great view of the Oktoberfest. At other times, views are not particularly inspiring.

Mass of beer

Oktoberfest's Astounding Stats

○ The biggest ever beer tent was the Bräurosl of 1913 which held a whopping 12,000 drinkers.

○ Munich's biggest bash of the year has been cancelled an amazing 24 times, mostly due to cholera epidemics and war.

○ If you are your party's nominated driver, don't think you're getting off lightly when it comes to the bill. A litre of water costs almost as much as a *Mass* of beer!

○ Some 90,000L of wine is supped over the 16 days of Wies'n frolics.

○ It takes around 10 weeks to erect the beer tents and five weeks to dismantle them.

○ Around 12,000 waitstaff are employed at Oktoberfest.

○ Around 75% of the Munich Red Cross' annual workload occurs during Oktoberfest.

Planning

Hotels book out very quickly and prices skyrocket, so reserve accommodation as early as you can (a year in advance). The festival is a 15-minute walk southwest of the Hauptbahnhof, and is served by its own U-Bahn station, Theresienwiese. Trams and buses have signs reading Zur Festwiese (literally 'to the Festival Meadow').

Survival Guide

Park-side cafe BARRY PACK/EYEEM/GETTY IMAGES ©

Before You Go

Book Your Stay

o Munich has the full range of accommodation options you would expect from a major city in Western Europe.

o Luxury hotels dot the centre, midrange places are clustered near the Hauptbahnhof.

o Room rates tend to be higher than in the rest of Bavaria, and they skyrocket during the Oktoberfest.

o Midrange accommodation is cheaper here than in other major European cities.

o During Oktoberfest try to find accommodation in other towns around Munich that have good rail connections to the Bavarian capital.

o Renting a *Ferien-wohnung* (furnished flat) for a week or longer is a sensible option for self-caterers, families and small groups.

o Bavaria has many hostels of both the indie and youth varieties.

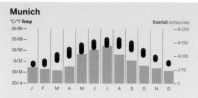

When to Go

o **Spring (Apr–Jun)** The shoulder seasons (spring and autumn) are the best time to visit, though the weather can still be nippy in April.

o **Summer (Jul & Aug)** Locals head for the hills but visitors arrive in their thousands. Temperatures are at their highest and the city centre can get muggy. Festival season.

o **Autumn (Sep & Oct)** Colourful time to be in Munich but avoid late September and early October unless visiting Oktoberfest when accommodation is impossible to find.

o **Winter (Nov–Mar)** Expect subzero temperatures and snow. December is Christmas-market time.

Useful Websites

Lonely Planet (lonely planet.com/munich) Recommendations and bookings.

Munich Tourist Office (www.muenchen.de) Maintains the most comprehensive and regularly updated list of accommodation options.

European Union (reopen.europa.eu) Current COVID-19 restrictions in the EU.

Best Budget

Pension Westfalia (www.pension-west falia.de) Family-run guesthouse near the Theresienwiese.

Tent (www.the-tent. com) Floor space in the Tent is the cheapest sleep in Munich.

Wombats City Hostel Munich (www. wombats-hostels.com) The city centre's best hostel.

Best Midrange

Hotel Cocoon (www.hotel-cocoon.de) Ultra-cool design near the Hauptbahnhof.

Hotel Laimer Hof (www.laimerhof.de) Some 23 reasonably priced rooms near Schloss Nymphenburg.

La Maison (www.hotel-la-maison.com) Cool design pad in Schwabing.

Hotel Marienbad (www.hotelmarienbad.de) Old-fashioned but stylish hotel in Maxvorstadt.

Hotel Ritzi (www.hotel-ritzi.de) Possibly Munich's quirkiest place to sleep.

Best Top End

Bayerischer Hof (www.bayerischerhof.de) Luxury and tradition hand in hand in the Altstadt.

Cortiina (www.cortiina.com) A favourite with design-minded travellers with cash to splash.

Flushing Meadows (www.flushingmeadowshotel.com) Some 11 rooms reflecting the vision of a locally known personality.

Louis Hotel (www.louis-hotel.com) The 72 rooms here are studies in elegant sophistication.

Hotel Mandarin Oriental Munich (www.mandarinoriental.com) Possibly Munich's most luxurious offering.

Arriving in Munich

Munich Airport

Munich Airport (MUC; ☎089-975 00; www.munich-airport.de), aka Flughafen Franz-Josef Strauss, is second in importance only to Frankfurt for international and domestic connections. The main carrier is Lufthansa, but over 80 other companies operate from the airport's two runways, from major carriers such as British Airways and Emirates to minor operations such as Luxair and Air Malta.

S-Bahn S1 and S8 link the airport to the Hauptbahnhof. The trip costs €10,80, takes about 40 minutes and runs every 20 minutes almost 24 hours a day.

Bus The Lufthansa Airport Bus shuttles at 20-minute intervals between the airport and Arnulfstrasse, next to the Hauptbahnhof, between 5.15am and 7.55pm. The trip takes about 45 minutes and costs €10.50 (return €17).

Hauptbahnhof (Main Train Station)

Train connections from Munich to destinations in Bavaria are excellent and there are also numerous services from more distant cities within Germany and around Europe. All services pull in at the **Hauptbahnhof** (Central Station) in the east of the city centre.

Public Transport The Hauptbahnhof is linked to the rest of the city by S-Bahn, bus and tram. All S-Bahn lines pass through it.

Zentraler Omnibusbahnhof (ZOB)

The **Zentraler Omnibusbahnhof** (Central Bus Station, ZOB;

www.muenchen-zob.de;
Arnulfstrasse 21; S Hackerbrücke) handles the vast
majority of internation-
al and domestic coach
services. There's a
Eurolines/Touring
office, a supermarket
and various eateries
on the 1st floor; buses
arrive at ground level.

The main operator
out of the ZOB is now
low-cost coach com-
pany **Flixbus** (☎ 030 300
137 300; www.flixbus.com;
Zentraler Omnibusbahnhof,
Arnulfstrasse 21), which
links Munich to count-
less destinations across
Germany and beyond.

S-Bahn The nearest S-
Bahn station to the ZOB
is Hackerbrücke.

Allgäu Airport

Only one major airline
from the UK doesn't
use Munich's main
airport – Ryanair flies
into Memmingen's
Allgäu Airport (FMM;
☎ 08331-984 2000; www.
allgaeu-airport.de; Am
Flughafen 35, Memmingen),
125km to the west.

Bus The **Allgäu
Airport Express** (www.
aaexpress.de; Arnulf-
strasse; €20, prebooked
online €15) leaves from
Arnulfstrasse at the

Hauptbahnhof, making
the trip up to seven
times a day. The jour-
ney takes one hour 40
minutes and the fare is
€13 (return €19.50).

Nuremberg Airport

Good transport links
between Bavaria's two
biggest cities makes
Nuremberg Airport
(NUE; ☎ 0911-937 00;
www.airport-nuernberg.de;
Flughafenstrasse) a feasi-
ble option and often a
cheaper one.

Train Services run
twice hourly to Mu-
nich's Hauptbahnhof
(€40 and €60, one
hour). The airport and
the train station are
linked by U-Bahn.

Getting Around

S-Bahn

○ The backbone of Mu-
nich's public transport
system (MVV; www.mvv-
muenchen.de) reaches
out into the suburbs and
beyond.

○ All S-Bahn trains fol-
low the Stammstrecke

(central line) through
central Munich.

○ Services run almost 24
hours a day (approxi-
mately 4am to 1am).

○ Most convenient mode
of transport for getting
to/from the airport.

Tram

○ Trams link the centre
with the inner suburbs.

○ Good for short and
medium journeys.

○ Best way to reach
Nymphenburg.

U-Bahn

○ The modern under-
ground system serves
the city centre and the
inner suburbs.

○ Operates almost 24
hours a day.

○ Good for medium
journeys such as to
the Olympic Park and
Haidhausen.

Bus

○ Operate mostly in the
suburbs linking residen-
tial areas and villages
to S-Bahn and U-Bahn
stations.

○ Only bus 100, which
passes many of the
city's museums, is of
any use to visitors.

Bicycle

o Munich has one of the best networks of cycling trails in Europe which locals use to commute to work.

o Cycle hire is easy to arrange. Try **Radius Tours** (☏089-543 487 7740; www.radiustours. com; Arnulfstrasse 3, Hauptbahnhof; ⊙8.30am-8pm; ☐Hauptbahnhof, ⓤHauptbahnhof, ⓢHauptbahnhof) at the Hauptbahnhof.

o Bikes can be taken on the S-Bahn but not from 6am to 9am and 4pm to 6pm Monday to Friday (rush hour). All bikes need a ticket.

o Helmets are not legally required but are, of course, recommended.

o Munich's commuters travel very fast along cycle paths – make sure you don't dally too much.

Car & Motorcycle

o Driving in central Munich can be a trial; many of the streets are one way or pedestrian only, ticket enforcement is Orwellian and parking is a nightmare.

o Car parks (indicated on the tourist-office map) charge about €1.70 to €2.20 per hour.

o When bringing your own vehicle to Germany, you need a valid driving licence, your car registration certificate and proof of insurance.

o Equipment you need to have in your car by law includes a first-aid kit, spare bulbs and a warning triangle.

o Between November and May make sure your vehicle is fitted with winter tyres and carry snow chains in the boot. Spiked tyres are prohibited.

Essential Information

Accessible Travel

Generally speaking, Munich caters well for the needs of the *Behinderte* (disabled), especially the wheelchair-bound. You'll find access ramps and/or lifts in many public buildings, including train stations, museums,

theatres and cinemas. New hotels and some renovated establishments have lifts and rooms with extra-wide doors and spacious, accessible bathrooms. Nearly all trains are accessible, and the city's buses and U-Bahns are becoming increasingly so. Seeing-eye dogs are allowed on all forms of public transport.

Many local and regional tourism offices have special brochures for people with disabilities, although usually in German. Good general resources include the following.

Deutsche Bahn Mobility Service Centre (☏0180 651 2512; www.bahn.com) Train-access information and route-planning assistance.

German National Tourism Office (www. germany.travel) Your first port of call, with inspirational information in English. Click on 'Travel Barrier Free'.

Munich for Physically Challenged Tourists (www.munich. de) Searching the official Munich tourism website will produce gigabytes of info on everything for travellers with disabilities, from Oktoberfest to local clubs and organisations to special ride services.

Natko (www.natko.de) Central clearing house for enquiries about barrier-free travel in Germany.

Business Hours

Banks 8.30am–4pm Monday to Friday, limited opening Saturday

Restaurants 11am–11pm

Cafes 7.30am–7pm

Bars and Clubs 6pm–1am minimum, some clubs open until 6am or 7am at weekends

Shops 9.30am–8pm Monday to Saturday

Discount Cards

The **Munich City Tour Card** (www.citytourcard-muenchen.com; one/three days €12.90/24.90) includes all public transport in the *Innenraum* (Munich city – zones 1 to 4, marked white on transport maps) and discounts of between 10% and 50% for over 80 attractions, tours, eateries and theatres. These include the Residenz, the BMW Museum and the Bier & Oktoberfestmuseum. The card is available for purchase at some hotels as well as at tourist offices, Munich public transport authority (MVV) offices and U-Bahn, S-Bahn and DB vending machines.

Electricity

Type C
230V/50Hz

Type F
230V/50Hz

LGBTIQ+ Travellers

Homosexuality is legal in Bavaria, but the scene, even in Munich, is tiny compared to, say, Berlin or Cologne. Homosexuality is widely accepted, and LGBTIQ+ travellers will experience no hostility in the capital. There are websites aplenty, but most are in German only. Try www.gay-web.de or, for women, www.lesarion.de. The **Schwules Kommunikations und Kulturzentrum** (☑089-856 346 400; www.subonline.org; Müllerstrasse 14; ☺7-11pm Sun-Thu, to midnight Fri, 8pm-1am Sat; ☒Müllerstrasse) in the city centre is a gay information agency. Lesbians can also turn to **Le Tra** (☎089-725 4272; www.letra.de; Angertorstrasse 3; ⏱2.30-5pm Mon & Wed; 🚇Müllerstrasse).

Money

○ Germany is one of the 17 countries in the EU that uses the euro as its national currency. No other currency is accepted.

○ Euros come in seven notes (five, 10, 20, 50, 100, 200 and 500 euros) and eight coins (one and two euro coins, and one, two, five, 10, 20 and 50 cent coins). You're unlikely ever to set eyes on a 200 or 500 euro note.

○ Exchange money at airports, some banks and currency exchange offices, such as Reisebank, American Express and TravelEx. In rural areas, such facilities are rare, so make sure you have plenty of cash.

ATMs

ATMs widely available. Credit and debit cards accepted at most hotels and shops but not all restaurants.

ATMs are ubiquitous, accessible 24/7 and the easiest and quickest way to obtain cash. However not all machines take all cards. Check with your bank or credit-card company about fees.

Cash

Bavaria is still very much a cash culture and making sure you have ample supply of the stuff will avoid embarrassing situations, such as trying to pay for a beer in a pub or a sausage at the railway station with your credit card. Even at the supermarket, cashiers (and the queue behind you) can still get a bit huffy if you don't have readies, especially when spending small sums.

Tipping

You could get through an entire trip around southern Germany without giving a single tip. Few service industry employees expect them, though most still appreciate a little extra when it comes to their way.

Hotels Generally €1 per bag.

Pubs Leave a little small change for the barman.

Restaurants Round up the bill to the nearest €5 (or €10) if you were satisfied with service.

Taxis Round up to the nearest €5 so the driver doesn't have to hunt for change.

Toilet Attendants Unless a price list states exact rates, €0.50 is about right.

Exchange Rates

Australia	A$1	€0.63
Canada	C$1	€0.68
Japan	¥100	€0.76
New Zealand	NZ$1	€0.58
UK	UK£1	€1.18
USA	US$1	€0.87

For current exchange rates see www.xe.com

Credit Cards

A piece of plastic can be vital in emergencies and occasionally also useful for phone or internet bookings. Avoid getting cash on your credit card via ATMs since fees are steep and you'll be charged interest immediately (in other words, there's no grace period as with purchases).

Dos & Don'ts

Southern Germans are a pretty rigid bunch, with elderly people in particular expecting lots of set behaviour and stock phrases. It's easy to make a mistake, but the following should help you avoid red-faced moments.

On the phone Always give your name first when you are making a call or receiving one. Not to do so is seen as impolite.

Greetings Begin every new interaction with locals with a hearty *Grüss Gott*, the southern German for hello (in the rest of Germany it's *Guten Tag*).

Touchy subject It's probably best to avoid conversations about Munich's role in the rise of the Nazis, especially with older people.

Punctuality When meeting up, punctuality is appreciated – never arrive more than 15 minutes late

At the table Tucking in before the *'Guten Appetit'* starting gun is fired is regarded as bad manners. When drinking wine, the toast is *'Zum Wohl'*, with beer it's *'Prost'*.

Report lost or stolen cards to the following:

American Express
☎ 069 9797 1000

MasterCard
☎ 0800 819 1040

Visa ☎ 0800 814 9100

Public Holidays

Businesses and offices are closed on the following public holidays:

Neujahrstag (New Year's Day) 1 January

Heilige Drei Könige (Epiphany) 6 January

Ostern (Easter) March/April – Good Friday, Easter Sunday and Easter Monday

Maifeiertag (Labour Day) 1 May

Christi Himmelfahrt (Ascension Day) 40 days after Easter

Pfingsten (Whitsun/Pentecost) mid-May to mid-June – Whit Sunday and Whit Monday

Fronleichnam (Corpus Christi) 10 days after Pentecost

Mariä Himmelfahrt (Assumption Day, Bavaria only) 15 August

Tag der Deutschen Einheit (Day of German Unity) 3 October

Weihnachtstag (Christmas Day) 25 December

Sankt Stephanstag (Boxing/St Stephen's Day) 26 December

Safe Travel

During Oktoberfest crime and staggering drunks are major problems, especially around the Hauptbahnhof. It's no joke: drunks in a crowd trying to make their way home can get violent, and there are around 100 cases of assault every year. Leave early or stay cautious – if not sober – yourself.

Strong and unpredictable currents make cooling off in

the Eisbach creek in the Englischer Garten more dangerous than it looks. Exercise extreme caution; there have been deaths.

Fast-moving bikes in central Munich are a menace. Make sure you don't wander onto bike lanes, especially when waiting to cross the road and when alighting from buses and trams.

Toilets

o Men's toilets are marked 'Herren' (or just 'H'), the ladies' 'Damen' (or just 'D').

o Public toilets in Munich are almost non-existent. Instead use facilities in department stores, railway stations, markets, beer halls and other public places.

o Toilets are rarely free, and those at large railway stations can charge €1. At some facilities payment is by donation, thus you pay as much as you like. At others there's a price list.

o Sanifair toilets charge €0.70, but you receive a €0.50 voucher to spend in the establishment in which it is located.

This type of facility has spread in recent years from motorway service stations to other places such as department stores and train stations. Many jump the low barriers.

o Toilets are normally clean, well maintained and not of the squat variety, though some are of the slightly off-putting 'reverse bowl design', not common in the UK or US.

Tourist Information

Castles & Museums Infopoint (☎ 089-2101 4050; www.infopoint-museen-bayern.de; Alter Hof 1; ◷ 10am-6pm Mon-Sat; Ⓤ Marienplatz, Ⓢ Marienplatz) Central information point for museums and palaces throughout Bavaria.

Tourist Office Branches include **Hauptbahnhof** (☎ 089-21 800; www.muenchen.de; Bahnhofplatz 2; ◷ 9am-8pm Mon-Sat, 10am-6pm Sun; 🚆 Hauptbahnhof, Ⓤ Hauptbahnhof, Ⓢ Hauptbahnhof) and **Marienplatz** (☎ 089-2339 6500; www.muenchen.de; Marienplatz

2; ◷ 9am-7pm Mon-Fri, to 4pm Sat, 10am-2pm Sun; Ⓤ Marienplatz, Ⓢ Marienplatz).

Visas

Most EU nationals only need their national identity card or passport to enter, stay and work in Germany. Citizens of Australia, Canada, Israel, Japan, New Zealand, the UK and the US are among those countries that need only a valid passport (no visa) if entering as tourists for up to three months within a six-month period. Passports should be valid for at least another six months from the planned date of departure from Germany

Nationals from other countries need a socalled Schengen Visa, named after the 1995 Schengen Agreement that enables passport controls between most countries in the EU to be abolished. For full details, see www.auswaertiges-amt.de or check with a German consulate in your country.

Responsible Travel

Shop Authentic & Sustainable

Munich provides lots of opportunities to buy high-quality second-hand clothes, as well as used traditional costume for Oktoberfest. **Pick n Weight** (https://picknweight. de/pages/munich), Holareidulijö (p79) and **Oxfam** (www.oxfam. de) are just some of the places you can pick up preloved garb.

Public Transport

Munich has a superb public transport system. There really is no need to rent a car in these parts, even if you are planning a daytrip out of the city – trains and buses can get you anywhere.

Bike It!

You only have to step out of the main entrance of the Hauptbahnhof to see that Munich takes pedalling seriously. Bike hire is easy, cycle lanes and other infrastructure ubiquitous and traffic rules geared towards two-wheelers.

Language

It's easy to pronounce German because almost all sounds are also found in English – just read our pronunciation guides as if they were English and you'll be understood.

In German, word stress falls mostly on the first syllable – in our pronunciation guides the stressed syllable is indicated with italics.

Note that German has polite and informal forms for 'you' (*Sie* and *du* respectively). When addressing people you don't know well, use the polite form. In this language guide, polite forms are used, unless you've given both options. Also note that (m/f) indicates masculine and feminine forms.

To enhance your trip with a phrasebook, visit lonelyplanet.com.

Basics

Hello.
Guten Tag. goo·ten taak

Goodbye.
Auf Wiedersehen. owf vee·der·zey·en

How are you? (pol/inf)
Wie geht es Ihnen/dir? vee gayt es ee·nen/deer

Fine, thanks.
Danke, gut. dang·ke goot

Please.
Bitte. bi·te

Thank you.
Danke. dang·ke

Excuse me.
Entschuldigung. ent·shul·di·gung

Sorry.
Entschuldigung. ent·shul·di·gung

Yes./No.
Ja./Nein. yah/nain

Do you speak (English)?
Sprechen Sie Englisch? shpre·khen zee eng·lish

I (don't) understand.
Ich verstehe (nicht). ikh fer·shtay·e (nikht)

Eating & Drinking

I'm a vegetarian. (m/f)
Ich bin Vegetarier/ ikh bin ve·ge·tah·ri·er/
Vegetarierin. ve·ge·tah·ri·e·in

Cheers!
Prost! prawst

That was delicious!
Das war sehr lecker! das vahr zair le·ker

Please bring the bill.
Die Rechnung, bitte. dee rokh·nung bi·te

I'd like ...
Ich möchte ... ikh merkh·te ...

a coffee	*einen Kaffee*	ai·nen ka·fay
a glass of wine	*ein Glas Wein*	ain glas wain
a table for two	*einen Tisch für zwei Personen*	ai·nen tish für tsvai per·zaw·nen
two beers	*zwei Bier*	tsvai beer

Shopping

I'd like to buy ...
Ich möchte ... kaufen. ikh merkh·te ... kow·fen

May I look at it?
Können Sie es ker·nen zee es
mir zeigen? meer tsai·gen

How much is it?
Wie viel kostet das? vee feel kos·tet das

That's too expensive.
Das ist zu teuer. das ist tsoo toy·er

Can you lower the price?
Können Sie mit ker·nen zee mit
dem Preis dem prais
heruntergehen? he·run·ter·gay·en

There's a mistake in the bill.
Da ist ein Fehler in dah ist ain fay·ler in
der Rechnung. dair rekh·nung

Emergencies

Help!
Hilfe! hil·fe

Call a doctor!
Rufen Sie roo·fen zee
einen Arzt! ai·nen artst

Call the police!
Rufen Sie roo·fen zee
die Polizei! dee po·li·tsai

I'm lost.
Ich habe ikh hah·be
mich verirrt. mikh fer·irt

I'm ill.
Ich bin krank. ikh bin krangk

Where's the toilet?
Wo ist die Toilette? vo ist dee to·a·le·te

Time

What time is it?
Wie spät ist es? vee shpayt ist es

It's (10) o'clock.
Es ist (zehn) Uhr. es ist (tsayn) oor

morning	*Morgen*	mor·gen
afternoon	*Nach-*	nahkh·
	mittag	mi·tahk
evening	*Abend*	ah·bent
yesterday	*gestern*	ges·tern

today	*heute*	hoy·te
tomorrow	*morgen*	mor·gen

Numbers

1	*eins*	ains
2	*zwei*	tsvai
3	*drei*	drai
4	*vier*	feer
5	*fünf*	fünf
6	*sechs*	zeks
7	*sieben*	zee·ben
8	*acht*	akht
9	*neun*	noyn
10	*zehn*	tsayn
100	*hundert*	hun·dert
1000	*tausend*	tow·sent

Transport & Directions

Where's ...?
Wo ist ...? vaw ist ...

What's the address?
Wie ist die vee ist dee
Adresse? a·dre·se

Can you show me (on the map)?
Können Sie es mir ker·nen zee es meer
(auf der Karte) (owf dair kar·te)
zeigen? tsai·gen

I want to go to ...
Ich mochte ikh merkh·te
nach ... fahren. nahkh ... fah·ren

What time does it leave?
Wann fährt es ab? van fairt es ap

What time does it arrive?
Wann kommt van komt
es an? es an

Does it stop at ...?
Hält es in ...? helt es in ...

I want to get off here.
Ich mochte hier ikh merkh·te heer
aussteigen. ows·shtai·gen

Behind the Scenes

Send Us Your Feedback

We love to hear from travellers – your comments help make our books better. We read every word, and we guarantee that your feedback goes straight to the authors. Visit **lonelyplanet.com/contact** to submit your updates and suggestions.

Note: We may edit, reproduce and incorporate your comments in Lonely Planet products such as guidebooks, websites and digital products, so let us know if you don't want your comments reproduced or your name acknowledged. For a copy of our privacy policy visit lonelyplanet.com/legal.

Marc's Thanks

Huge thanks goes out to Robert Leckel of München Tourismus for his invaluable assistance and great ideas. I'd also like to thank all the staff of Bavaria's excellent tourist offices for their help. Finally, many thanks to my wife for holding the fort while I was away researching.

Acknowledgements

Cover photograph: Olympiapark, Munich; Viacheslav Lopatin/Shutterstock ©

Back cover photograph: Pretzels, bratwurst and sauerkraut; George Dolgikh/Shutterstock ©

Photographs pp34–5 (from left): phillus, Nenad Nedomacki/Shutterstock ©; WestendGI, Foo'l loo, Thrll/Getty ©

This Book

This 2nd edition of Lonely Planet's *Pocket Munich* was updated by Marc Di Duca. Marc also researched and wrote the 1st edition. This guidebook was produced by the following:

Destination Editor
Niamh O'Brien

Senior Product Editors
Genna Patterson, Angela Tinson

Product Editors Barbara Delissen, Kate Mathews

Senior Cartographer
Valentina Kremenchutskaya

Book Designers Ania Bartoszek, Norma Brewer

Assisting Cartographer
Hunor Csutoros

Assisting Editors Joel Cotterell, Monique Perrin, Simon Williamson

Cover Researchers Gwen Cotter, Naomi Parker

Thanks to James Appleton, Grace Dobell, Mark Griffiths, Sonia Kapoor, Sandie Kestell

Index

See also separate subindexes for:

⊗ **Eating p159**
◉ **Drinking p159**
✪ **Entertainment p159**
🔒 **Shopping p159**

Sights 000
Map Pages **000**

Sights 000
Map Pages **000**

Our Writer

Marc Di Duca

A travel author for more than a decade, Marc has
worked for Lonely Planet in Siberia, Slovakia, Bavaria.
England, Ukraine, Austria, Poland, Croatia, Portugal,
Madeira and on the Trans-Siberian Railway, as well
as writing and updating tens of guides for other
publishers. When not on the road, Marc lives near
Mariánské Lázně in the Czech Republic with his wife
and two sons.

Published by Lonely Planet Global Limited
CRN 554153
2nd edition – Jul 2022
ISBN 978 1 78868 097 4
© Lonely Planet 2022   Photographs © as indicated 2022
10 9 8 7 6 5 4 3 2 1
Printed in Singapore

Although the authors and Lonely Planet
have taken all reasonable care in preparing
this book, we make no warranty about the
accuracy or completeness of its content and,
to the maximum extent permitted, disclaim
all liability arising from its use.